S0-BDA-115

Kye Kim's

Simply Delicious One Course Meals

Kye Kim's
Simply Delicious One Course Meals

케이 킴의 손쉽고 맛깔스러운 원 코스요리

By Kye Kim

Recipe anecdotes contributed by Michelle Kim Vaughan

북하우스엔

This book is dedicated to the men in my life :
my husband, Chin Myung, my son, Michael and my son-in-law, Brendan.
Nothing gives me more pleasure than cooking for all of you.

foreword

This book is very special to me because this is a unique and special time in my life. I am turning sixty very soon, and for the first time I feel I am truly aware of who I am as a person and what makes me happy. As a celebration of that sense of self, I made a decision to make this book a true reflection of what I like to eat. However, as I began my work I realized that my true inspiration comes from my desire to share what I love with my husband and children. The food that I make is so much more than a form of sustenance; it is an expression of my love. My love goes into the formation of every dish and writing cookbooks is a way for me to teach my children not only to recreate the food that they grew up eating at home, but to feel a little of the love that I put into everything I make for them.

Now, my children all have full-time jobs and very little free time. They always tell me that after a long day of work, the last thing they want to do is eat take-out food every night, or in my daughter's case, a bowl of cereal. What they really want is to eat a home-cooked meal. Since they don't have me at home to cook for them, I decided the next best thing was to help them create that meal for themselves. With that in mind, whenever I lacked inspiration, I would put myself in their place and imagine what I would most like to eat in that moment. So in that way, this book became not only a reflection of myself, but a reflection of how I share my love with others.

Now, I realize that not everyone has lot of cooking experience and when your free time is precious, you may not have the energy to make something that is complicated or time consuming. It was very important to me to not only share recipes for delicious food, but to make that food accessible to people who live a modern life. So, for all of you busy people out there, this book is for you. It will teach you how to make a quick, easy, one-course dinner or lunch that will be both healthful and delicious. This way, no matter how chaotic life gets, you can fix a meal with a bit of mother's love for yourself and others to enjoy at home.

I would like to mention my daughter, Michelle, who wrote a bit of narration or an anecdote for each of the recipes. She tested many of them as a real-life example of the type of person this book is meant for; a young professional with a full-time job, and I'd like to thank her for her work. We had a really great time working on this book together, and I will always cherish the memories from the experience. I'd like to thank my best friend Laura Baur, who helped me through every step of this process, whether it was proofreading, design, or just providing me with emotional support. I would also like to thank God who makes all things possible, and my publisher, who gave me the opportunity to write this book in the first place. Finally, of course, I would like to thank my family, who provide the inspiration for all of my work.

contents

part I beef

part 2 chicken

part 3 noodles & rice

part 4 pork

part 5 seafood

part 6 vegetarian

This section of the book is probably the most useful and versatile when it comes to saving time for meal preparation. All of the recipes in this book teach you techniques that can be used in combination with different ingredients. This means that learning a recipe is not just learning to make one meal; it is learning skills that give you the building blocks to make several different meals. The technique I find most invaluable is how to make a good sauce. All of the sauces below can be made ahead of time and combined with whatever you have on hand in the refrigerator. If you prep your vegetables, proteins, and sauces over the weekend, you can use these ingredients however you wish during the week and still have a delicious, home-cooked meal in a very short amount of time. All of the sauces below last between 1 and 2 weeks stored in an airtight container in the refrigerator.

이 장에서는 요리 준비에 드는 시간을 줄이는 아주 유용한 방법을 알려드리려고 합니다. 이 책에 수록된 레시피를 응용해서 다른 재료를 가지고도 요리할 수 있는 실력을 기를 수 있답니다. 레시피를 배운다는 것은 단순히 한 가지 요리를 만드는 법을 습득한다는 것이 아니라 배운 레시피를 응용해서 여러 종류의 다른 요리들을 만들 수 있는 기초를 다진다는 의미일 겁니다. 제가 배운 가장 소중한 비법은 바로 훌륭한 소스를 만드는 것입니다. 지금 냉장고에 있는 재료로 미리 만들어두었다가 쓸 수 있는 소스 말이죠. 주말에 채소나 육류, 소스 등을 준비해두었다가 주중에 언제든지 맛있는 가정식을 순식간에 만들어 낼 수 있답니다. 다음의 소스들은 밀폐용기에 넣어 냉장고에 보관하면 1~2주 정도 거뜬하게 사용할 수 있습니다.

Basic Sauce

- **5 tablespoons vinegar**
- **4 tablespoons sugar**
- **1 tablespoon salt**

Possible Uses As a marinade for sushi rice or as a base for dipping sauces or salad dressings.

베이식 소스 • 식초 5큰술 • 설탕 4큰술 • 소금 1큰술
잘 섞어서 보관했다가 초밥에 단촛물로 쓰거나 딥핑 소스나 샐러드 드레싱 등의 각종 소스를 만들 때 섞어 쓰면 좋다.

Bibim Sauce

- 4 tablespoons Korean hot pepper paste (gochujang)
- 3 tablespoons sugar
- 3 tablespoons vinegar
- I tablespoon lemon juice
- ½ teaspoon garlic, minced
- I tablespoon toasted sesame seeds

Possible Uses As a sauce for bibimbap or hwe dup bap, as a dressing for cold noodles such as bibim nengmyun, as a dipping sauce for vegetables or thinly sliced grilled pork belly.

초고추장 · 고추장 4큰술 · 설탕 3큰술 · 식초 3큰술 · 레몬즙 1큰술
· 다진 마늘 ½작은술 · 볶은 깨 1큰술
비빔밥, 회덮밥, 비빔냉면 등에 사용하거나 채소나 데친
오징어, 삼겹살 등을 찍어 먹어도 좋다.

Bulgogi Sauce

- 3 tablespoons brown sugar
- 6 tablespoons cold water
- 3 tablespoons soy sauce
- I tablespoon rice wine
- I teaspoon toasted sesame seeds
- I tablespoon sesame oil
- ¼ teaspoon ground black pepper
- I tablespoon green onion, chopped
- I teaspoon minced garlic
- I+ ½ teaspoon ginger juice
  (Ginger juice can be created by grating ginger finely over a bowl and collecting the resulting juices.)
- I teaspoon cornstarch + I tablespoon water

Combine brown sugar, water, green onion, garlic, ginger juice, soy sauce, rice wine, sesame seeds, sesame oil and black pepper in a saucepan and bring to a boil, stirring constantly. Dissolve cornstarch in I tablespoon of cold water and add to the sauce. Stir constantly to allow the sauce to thicken.

Possible Uses As a sauce for beef, pork, chicken and vegetables stir-fries or as a basting sauce for grilled tofu.

불고기 소스 · 흑설탕 3큰술 · 물 6큰술 · 간장 3큰술 · 청주 1큰술
· 볶은 깨 1작은술 · 참기름 1큰술 · 후추 ¼작은술 · 다진 파 1큰술 ·
다진 마늘 1작은술 · 생강즙 1 ½작은술 · 전분 1작은술 + 물 1큰술,
잘 섞어둔다
작은 냄비에 전분을 제외한 소스 재료들을 넣고 잘 저으면
서 끓인다. 소스 재료가 끓어 오르면 녹말물을 넣고 골고루
잘 저어 걸죽하게 만든다. 쇠고기, 돼지고기, 닭고기와 채
소볶음이나 두부구이 등에 소스로 사용하면 좋다.

Dipping Sauce

- I tablespoon soy sauce
- ½ tablespoon sugar
- ½ tablespoon rice vinegar

Possible Uses As a dipping sauce for jun, pyunsoo, milsaam, or mandu.

초간장 (전, 편수, 밀쌈) • 간장 1큰술 • 설탕 ½큰술 • 식초 ½큰술
전, 편수, 밀쌈 또는 만두 등을 찍어 먹는 딥핑 소스로 좋다.

Soy Dipping Sauce

- 3 tablespoons basic sauce
  (Basic sauce is made of 5 parts vinegar to 4 parts
  sugar to I part salt.)
- 4 tablespoons chicken stock
- 2 tablespoons soy sauce
- I teaspoon prepared Asian hot mustard
- I tablespoon toasted sesame seeds
- I tablespoon green onion, chopped

Possible Uses As a dressing for hot or cold noo-dles, as a dressing for salad, as a dipping sauce for cooked meats, such as in Shabu Shabu.

간장 소스 • 베이식 소스 3큰술(식초5 : 설탕4 : 소금1) • 닭육수 4큰
술 • 간장 2큰술 • 갠 겨자 1작은술 • 볶은 깨 1큰술 • 다진 파 1큰술
샤부샤부에 딥핑 소스로 사용하거나 여러 가지 국수요리
또는 샐러드 드레싱으로 이용하면 좋다.

Spicy Marinade for Meat

- 2 ½ pounds protein
- 4 tablespoons honey
- 4 tablespoons water
- 1 tablespoon mirin
- 2 tablespoons Korean hot pepper paste (gochujang)
- 1 ½ tablespoons soy sauce
- 1 tablespoon chopped green onion
- 2 teaspoons minced garlic
- ¼ teaspoon black pepper
- 1 tablespoon toasted sesame seeds
- 3 tablespoons sesame oil

Possible Uses As a marinade for pork ribs, chicken, or white fish. One recipe makes enough marinade for 2 ½ pounds of protein.

매운 고기양념 • 돼지갈비 또는 돼지고기, 닭고기, 흰살생선 2 ½ 파운드 • 꿀 4큰술 • 물 4큰술 • 맛술 1큰술
• 고추장 2큰술 • 간장 1 ½큰술 • 다진 파 1큰술 • 다진 마늘 2작은술
• 후추 ¼작은술 • 볶은 깨 1큰술 • 참기름 3큰술
돼지갈비 또는 돼지고기, 닭고기, 흰살생선 등을 재는 데 사용하면 좋다. 분량의 소스로 1킬로그램 정도의 고기를 잴 수 있다.

Spicy Pepper Sauce

- 1 green onion (white part only), chopped
- 1 mini red pepper, cored and seeded, chopped
- 1 jalapeño pepper, cored and seeded, chopped
- 2 tablespoons soy sauce
- 2 tablespoons rice vinegar
- 1 tablespoon sugar
- 1 tablespoon sesame oil
- 2 tablespoons water

Possible Uses As a salad dressing, drizzled over cold cooked beef and vegetables, or as a marinade for shrimp.

매콤한 페퍼 소스 • 파(흰 부분) 1대, 다진다 • 미니 홍파프리카 1개,
씨를 빼고 잘게 썬다 • 매운 풋고추 2개, 씨를 빼고 잘게 썬다
• 간장 2큰술 • 식초 2큰술 • 설탕 1큰술 • 참기름 1큰술 • 물 2큰술
로스구이처럼 익힌 쇠고기와 채소를 곁들인 요리에 드레싱으로 사용하거나 새우를 양념하여 샐러드 그린과 같이 내도 좋다.

Soy Marinade for Meat

- I pound protein
- I ½ tablespoons brown sugar
- I ½ tablespoons water
- 2 teaspoons mirin
- 2 ½ tablespoons soy sauce
- I ½ teaspoons minced garlic
- I tablespoon chopped green onion
- ½ teaspoon ginger juice
- ¼ teaspoon black pepper
- 2 teaspoons toasted sesame seeds
- I tablespoon sesame oil

Possible Uses As a marinade for protein used in bulgogi or galbigui, such as beef, chicken or pork.

고기 양념 • 얇게 썬 고기 1파운드 • 흑설탕 1 ½큰술 • 물 1 ½큰술 • 맛술 2작은술 • 간장 2 ½큰술 • 다진 마늘 1 ½작은술 • 다진 파 1큰 술 • 생강즙 ½작은술 • 후추 ¼작은술 • 볶은 깨 2작은술 • 참기름 1 큰술

불고기, 갈비구이, 닭불고기, 돼지불고기 등을 잴 때 사용 하면 좋다.

Sweet and Sour Sauce

- I cup vegetable broth or water
- I tablespoon canola oil
- I teaspoon garlic, chopped
- I teaspoon ginger, chopped
- 2 tablespoons soy sauce
- 5 tablespoons brown sugar
- 2 tablespoons rice vinegar
- I tablespoon cornstarch +
  I tablespoon water, mixed well

Mix together all of the ingredients for the Sweet and Sour Sauce except for the cornstarch and water mixture. Heat a small thick-bottomed pot over high heat. Add the sauce mixture and stir until it begins to boil. Add cornstarch and water mixture and continue to stir until the sauce thickens.

Possible Uses As a sauce for cooked beef, pork, fish, chicken or tofu, as a sauce for fried chicken or pork, or drizzled over warm, roasted vegetables.

탕수육 소스 • 채소국물(또는 물) 1컵 • 카놀라유 1큰술 • 다진 마늘 1작은술 • 다진 생강 1작은술 • 간장 2큰술 • 흑설탕 5큰술 • 식초 2큰 술 • 전분 1큰술 + 물 1큰술, 잘 섞어둔다

녹말 1큰술과 물 1큰술을 섞어 녹말물을 만들어놓는다. 물 녹말물을 뺀 소스 재료를 잘 섞어놓는다. 두꺼운 냄비에 섞 어둔 소스 재료를 넣고 저으면서 센 불에서 끓인다. 소스가 끓기 시작하면 녹말물을 넣고 계속 저으면서 걸죽하게 만 든다. 쇠고기, 돼지고기, 생선, 닭, 두부를 튀겨 소스를 입 히거나 구운 채소 위에 뿌려 먹으면 좋다.

Naengchae Sauce

- 5 tablespoons basic sauce
- 1 tablespoon sesame oil
- 1 teaspoon minced garlic
- ¼ teaspoon freshly ground black pepper

Possible Uses As a salad dressing, a spicy, tangy dressing for steamed seafood, a dipping sauce for dumplings or as a dressing for a cold noodle dish.

냉채 샐러드 소스 • 베이식 소스 5큰술 • 참기름 1큰술 • 다진 마늘 1 작은술 • 후추 ¼작은술

각종 샐러드 드레싱, 매콤하고 톡 쏘는 해물 냉채 소스, 만 두 등을 찍어 먹는 소스, 비빔국수 등에 사용할 수 있다.

Teriyaki Sauce

- ¼ cup soy sauce • ¼ cup mirin
- ¼ cup chicken stock or water
- 2 teaspoons fresh ginger, grated
- 3 tablespoons brown sugar
- 1 teaspoon garlic, minced
- 1 teaspoon cornstarch
- 1 tablespoon cold water

Combine chicken stock or water, soy sauce, brown sugar, mirin, garlic and ginger in a saucepan and bring to a boil, stirring constantly. Dissolve cornstarch in ¼ cup of cold water and add to sauce. Stir constantly until the sauce thickens. If the sauce is too thick add a little water to thin it out.

Possible Uses As a marinade or basting sauce for chicken, salmon, beef, or pork or a dressing for warm steamed vegetables.

데리야키 소스 • 간장 ¼컵 • 맛술 ¼컵 • 닭육수 또는 물 ¼컵 • 다 진 생강 2작은술 • 흑설탕 3큰술
• 다진 마늘 1작은술 • 전분 1작은술 + 물 1큰술, 잘 섞어둔다

냄비에 간장, 닭육수, 맛술, 흑설탕, 다진 마늘, 다진 생강 을 넣고 저으면서 끓인다. 소스가 끓기 시작하면 풀어놓은 녹말물을 넣고 잘 섞는다. 이때 소스가 너무 걸죽하면 물을 조금 넣어 농도를 조절한다. 닭고기, 연어, 쇠고기 또는 돼 지고기 등을 구운 다음 그 위에 데리야키 소스를 발라 다시 한 번 구워내면 맛있는 데리야키가 된다. 고기를 얇게 썰어 팬에 지지고 양파, 당근, 피망, 또는 데친 브로콜리 등과 데 리야키 소스를 넣어 살짝 볶아내도 좋다.

beef

Sukiyaki 스키야키

Sukiyaki is a fun departure from the everyday meal. The ingredients are typically cooked at the table in a deep skillet filled with simmering hot soup. Traditionally, each person chooses what they would like to eat from the skillet and dips the freshly cooked sukiyaki in a small bowl of beaten eggs. The egg mixture partially cooks and thickens into sauce-like coating that adds a savory richness to the meal. *Cook's Note: Be sure to wash the bok choy very carefully, as there tends to be a lot of dirt trapped between the leaves.

Ingredients

- ½ pound thinly sliced beef, cut into bite-size pieces
- 16 ounces hard tofu, cut into 1-inch cubes
- 4 shitake mushrooms, stems removed
- 1 medium onion, peeled and sliced into ½ inch thick slices
- 3 leaves napa cabbage, cut into bite size pieces
- 3 baby bok choy, washed and cut into 2-inch pieces
- 1 package enoki mushrooms with the bottoms trimmed
- 2 green onions, cut into 2-inch pieces • 4 ounces shirataki noodles
- 2 pasteurized eggs, lightly beaten (optional) • 1 tablespoon canola oil

Ingredients for Sauce

- 1 cup kombu stock • 2/3 cup rice wine
- ¼ cup soy sauce • 3 tablespoons sugar

Mix kombu stock, rice wine, soy sauce and sugar together in a small pot and bring to boil. Then lower the heat and simmer.

Arrange beef, tofu, vegetables and noodles on a large plate and place the plate on the table.

To make sukiyaki it is easiest to use an electric skillet that can be placed directly on the table. However, if you do not have an electric skillet, you can easily cook the sukiyaki just prior to eating and then bring the skillet to the table.

Heat a large, deep skillet over medium high heat, or set an electric skillet to 425 F.

Add canola oil to the skillet and heat. Add meat slices to the skillet and cook until browned. Pour half of the sauce into the skillet, move the meat to the corner of the skillet when well browned. Add the other vegetables, keeping each separate. As the sauce boils, skim the surface often to remove any foam and fat. Simmer until all of the ingredients are softened. As the liquid reduces, add more of the reserved sauce or hot water. Serve immediately.

Optional Step: Dip the cooked sukiyaki into the beaten eggs, withdraw quickly, and eat.

재료(2인분) • 쇠고기 등심 500g, 한입 크기로 얇게 저며 썬다 • 두부 한모, 사방 1인치 크기로 썰어 기름에 살짝 지진다 • 표고버섯 4개, 기둥을 떼고 위를 열십자로 무늬를 낸다 • 양파 1개, ½인치 두께로 썬다 • 배춧잎 3장, 한입 크기로 썬다 • 청경채 3개, 먹기 좋은 크기로 썬다 • 팽이버섯 1봉지, 밑동을 자르고 먹기 좋게 뜯어둔다 • 대파 2대, 어슷하게 썬다 • 실곤약 1묶음(4온스), 물에 헹궈 작게 돌돌 말아둔다 • 달걀 2개, 작은 그릇에 한 개씩 풀어둔다 • 카놀라유 1큰술

무쇠냄비나 전기팬을 달궈 기름을 바르고 고기를 넣어 볶은 후 채소, 버섯, 두부와 다시 국물 반 정도를 넣고 끓인다. 이때 떠오르는 거품을 제거해야 국물이 깔끔하다. 입맛에 맞춰 간장과 설탕으로 간을 조절하고 재료가 익으면 풀어놓은 달걀에 찍어 먹거나 간장소스에 찍어 먹는다. 불을 약하게 하여 끓이면서 재료를 추가해가며 익혀 먹는다.

다시 국물 재료 • 다시마 국물 1컵, 청주 ⅔컵, 간장 ¼컵, 설탕 3큰술

다시마 국물에 청주, 간장, 설탕을 넣고 약한 불에 끈기가 날 때까지 끓인다. 스키야키 국물은 간을 조금 달게 해야 맛있다.

Marinated Flank Steak and Pickle Ssam 프랭크 스테이크 통불고기 쌈

This recipe is easy to prepare in large quantities, and is a crowd pleaser, which makes it a great meal to prepare when you are having a lot of people over for dinner. The soy sauce pickles are a perfect complement to the steak, providing a cool, crunchy, salty counterpart to the warm grilled meat. They are also perfect to snack on when you are craving something salty. I often double or triple the recipe just to have some on hand.

Ingredients
• 2 pounds flank steak • 3 tablespoons brown sugar
• 4 tablespoons cold water • I tablespoon green onion, chopped
• 4 tablespoons soy sauce • I tablespoon mirin
• 2 teaspoons toasted sesame seeds • I tablespoon sesame oil
• ¼ teaspoon black pepper • I teaspoon garlic, minced • I teaspoon ginger juice

Accompaniments
• I cup soy sauce pickled vegetables • 2 cups cooked short-grain rice
• 2 heads of any kind of lettuce, separated, well washed and dried.

Combine green onion, soy sauce, mirin, sesame seeds, black pepper, ginger juice and garlic to make marinade in a separate bowl and set aside.

Stir together brown sugar and water until sugar is mostly dissolved. Pour sugar water mixture over the meat and mix until meat is well coated. Let sit for about 5 minutes. Pour marinade over the meat and mix until it is well coated. Then add sesame oil and mix again to coat.

Let meat marinate 30 minutes, or if you wish, you can marinate it overnight. Cook meat on a grill, or if you prefer you may cook it in a frying pan, but grilling is best.

Remove the steak to a platter and let it rest for 10 minutes. Slice steak into ¼ inch thick slices, being sure to cut the meat against the grain. Place slices of meat, soy sauce picked vegetables and rice onto lettuce and enjoy.

재료 • 쇠고기(프랭크 스테이크) 900g • 흑설탕 3큰술 • 물 4큰술 • 맛술 1큰술 • 간장 4큰술 • 다진 마늘 1작은술 • 생강즙 1작은술 • 다진 파 1큰술 • 후추 ¼작은술 • 볶은 깨 2작은술 • 참기름 1큰술 곁들이 음식 • 채소 장아찌 1컵 • 밥 2컵 • 상추 2송이, 잎을 떼서 깨끗이 씻어 물기를 뺀다

간장, 맛술, 파, 마늘, 볶은 깨, 후추, 생강즙을 잘 섞어 양념장을 만들어둔다. 그릇에 흑설탕과 물을 넣고 잘 섞는다. 설탕이 녹으면 고기에 부어 골고루 섞어 5분간 둔 다음 양념장을 넣고 고루 무친다. 양념이 골고루 스며들면 참기름을 넣어 다시 한 번 버무려 약 30분 정도 두었다가 뜨거운 그릴이나 프라이팬에 통으로 구워내어 10분 정도 식힌다. 익힌 쇠고기를 도톰하게 썰어 밥, 장아찌, 상추와 함께 낸다.

tip 1. 양념을 거름망에 걸러 건더기를 제거한 후 사용하면 더 깔끔한 불고기를 만들 수 있다. 2. 불고기를 재워 냉장고에 하룻밤 두었다가 구우면 양념이 잘 배어 좋다. 3. 불고기를 잴 때 흑설탕물을 잘 코팅해주면 윤이 나는 맛있는 불고기를 만들 수 있다.

Soy Sauce Pickled Vegetables 채소 간장 장아찌

Ingredients

- 1 onion, cut diagonally into 2 inch pieces
- 1 small daikon radish or about ⅓ of a large one, cut into 1 ½ by 1 ½ by ¼ inch rectangles
- 2 pickling cucumbers or baby English cucumbers, cut into round slices
- 2 jalapeño peppers, cut into round slices
- 1 chayote, seeds removed, cut into thin slices
- 2 celery stalks, cut into ½ inch slices on the bias
- 2 cups soy sauce • 2 cups sugar • 2 cups rice vinegar

Combine soy sauce, sugar and vinegar in a saucepan. Bring to a boil over medium heat, stirring to dissolve the sugar. Place the rest of the ingredients in a heat safe container and carefully pour the soy sauce mixture over the vegetables until they are covered. Cool and then refrigerate. These pickles will be ready to eat in 1~2 weeks.

재료 • 양파 1개, 2인치 길이로 얇게 썰어둔다 • 작은 무 1개 또는 큰 무 ⅓개, 사방 1.5인치로 0.25인치 두께로 썬다 • 피클용 오이 2개, 둥글고 얇게 썬다 • 매운 고추 2개, 둥글고 얇게 썬다 • 차요테 1개, 4등분하여 씨를 빼고 얇게 썬다 • 셀러리 2줄기, 0.5인치 크기로 어슷하게 썬다 간장물 재료 • 간장 2컵 • 설탕 2컵 • 식초 2컵

냄비에 간장, 설탕, 식초를 넣고 설탕이 잘 녹도록 저으면서 끓인다. 준비해둔 모든 재료들을 그릇에 담고 뜨거운 간장물을 재료가 잠기게 부어준다. 이때 작은 지퍼백에 물을 넣고 그 위에 놓아 푹 잠기게 눌러주면 좋다. 실온에서 일주일 정도 익히거나 냉장고에 넣어 2주 정도 익혀서 먹는다.

Bulgogi Rolls 불고기롤

This recipe is a playful take on bibimbap, with a few changes to spice things up. Many of the ingredients traditionally used in bibimbap proved to be unwieldy in the form of a roll, so my mom used spears of asparagus and bell pepper instead. The tender yet crisp vegetables provide a great texture contrast to the beef. For those cooks who like to save a little time, pouring the sauce over the cooked meat creates the taste of traditional bulgogi, without the long marinating time.

Ingredients

- 1 pound of beef, sirloin • ½ onion, thinly sliced
- 10 asparagus stalks, cut into thin strips 3 inches long
- 6 mini red bell peppers, cut into thin strips • 3 tablespoons canola oil • salt

Ingredients for Sauce

- 3 tablespoons brown sugar • 6 tablespoons cold water
- 1 tablespoon green onion, chopped • 3 tablespoons soy sauce
- 1 tablespoon rice wine • 1 teaspoon toasted sesame seeds
- 1 tablespoon sesame oil • ¼ teaspoon ground black pepper • 1 teaspoon minced garlic
- 1+ ½ teaspoon ginger juice
  (Ginger juice can be created by grating ginger root finely over a bowl and collecting the resulting juices.)
- 1 teaspoon cornstarch + 1 tablespoon water

Slice the sirloin into extremely thin slices. Combine brown sugar, water, green onion, garlic, ginger juice, soy sauce, rice wine, sesame seeds, sesame oil and black pepper in a saucepan and bring to a boil, stirring constantly. Dissolve cornstarch in 1 tablespoon of cold water and add to the sauce. Stir constantly to allow the sauce to thicken.

Quickly sauté prepared vegetables in vegetable oil until tender and sprinkle with a little salt to taste. Transfer to plate and let cool. Heat 1 tablespoon of vegetable oil in a frying pan and cook beef over high heat until evenly browned, about 1 minute per side. Remove from pan.

Lay cooked beef slices out on a large, flat surface (a large plate or cutting board will do.) Divide the cooked vegetables evenly among the pieces of meat, placing them vertically across each piece. Roll the beef up over the filling, creating small bundles. Heat 2 tablespoons of vegetable oil in a large frying pan over medium high heat. Add the bundles of beef and vegetables and pour the prepared sauce evenly over the rolls. Cook for an additional 1-2 minutes. Garnish with sesame seeds and chopped green onions. Serve warm.

재료(4인분) • 쇠고기 등심 1파운드 • 양파 ½개, 채 썬다 • 아스파라거스 10개, 3인치 길이로 잘라 채 썬다 • 붉은 파프리카 6개(또는 홍피망 1개), 채 썬다 • 소금 약간 • 카놀라유(부침용) 3큰술 소스 재료 • 흑설탕 3큰술 • 물 6큰술 • 간장 3큰술 • 청주 1작은술 • 볶은 깨 1작은술 • 참기름 1큰술 • 후추 ¼작은술 • 다진 파 1큰술 • 다진 마늘 1작은술 • 생강즙 1 ½작은술 • 전분 1작은술 + 물 1큰술. 잘 섞어둔다

쇠고기는 불고깃감으로 얇게 썰어두고, 작은 냄비에 전분과 물을 뺀 소스 재료를 넣고 잘 저으면서 끓인다. 소스 재료가 끓어오르면 전분과 물을 넣어 잘 섞어 꺼룩하게 만든다. 뜨겁게 달군 팬에 기름을 두르고 썰어놓은 채소를 색이 살도록 볶아 소금으로 살짝 밑간을 해서 접시에 옮겨놓는다. 프라이팬을 달구어 기름을 1큰술 두르고 썰어놓은 고기를 한 장씩 놓아 익혀둔다. 접시에 고기를 한 장씩 펴고 볶아놓은 채소를 넣어 돌돌 말아둔다. 큰 프라이팬을 불에 달군 후 기름 2큰술을 두르고 돌돌 말아둔 고기를 넣고, 그 위에 소스를 부어 1~2분 정도 지져 접시에 담는다. 볶은 깨와 다진 파로 장식하여 따뜻할 때 낸다.

Shabu Shabu Salad 샤부샤부 냉샐러드

I love Shabu Shabu, but it tends to be a bit protein heavy, and sometimes you want something on the lighter side. This recipe allows you to enjoy the same tender, juicy, slices of beef but combines them with raw, crispy vegetables, making an interesting and satisfying salad.

Ingredients

- ½ pound thinly sliced beef loin or ribeye • ¼ head iceberg lettuce, cut into thin strips pieces
- ½ red onion, sliced into thin strips • I cup soy bean sprouts, trimmed and boiled
- 3 radishes, thinly sliced • ½ cup radish sprouts

Ingredients for Broth

- 4 cups water • I tablespoon mirin
- 2 inch square of kombu • ¼ cup bonito flakes
- I teaspoon soy sauce • I teaspoon salt

Ingredients for Dressing

- 3 tablespoons basic sauce
  (Basic sauce is made of 5 parts vinegar to 4 parts sugar to I part salt.)
- 4 tablespoons beef broth
- 2 tablespoons soy sauce
- I tablespoons toasted sesame seeds
- I teaspoon prepared Asian hot mustard

Mix together all ingredients for the dressing and set aside. Place the 4 cups of water in a large saucepan. Wipe down kombu with a damp paper towel and add it to the saucepan, letting it soak in the water for about 10 minutes. Add soy sauce, bring to a boil, and then turn off the heat. Add bonito flakes and leave for 15 minutes. Strain the liquid and return to the pot. Bring liquid to a boil.

Fill a medium bowl with ice water and set aside. Bring the broth to a boil and add beef slices in one by one. When beef slices are cooked, immediately transfer them to ice water to chill and drain off excess water.

Arrange the vegetables and cooked beef on a serving platter. Drizzle the dressing over the top of the salad or serve on the side as a dipping sauce.

재료 • 쇠고기(샤부샤부용) ½ 파운드 • 양상추 ¼개 • 적양파 ½개 • 콩나물 1컵 • 래디시 3개 • 무순 ½컵 육수 재료 • 물 4컵 • 맛술 1큰술 • 다시마 (사방 5cm) 1장 • 가쓰오부시 ¼컵 • 간장 1작은술 • 소금 1작은술 간장 소스 재료 • 베이식 소스 3큰술(식초5 : 설탕4 : 소금1) • 육수 4큰술 • 간장 2큰 술 • 볶은 깨 1큰술 • 겨자 1작은술

냄비에 다시마, 물, 맛술을 넣고 불에 올려 끓어오르면 가쓰오부시를 넣고 불을 끈 후 15분쯤 후에 걸러내 육수를 만든다. 끓는 육수에 준비한 쇠고기를 넣어 살짝 데쳐 얼음물에 넣어 식혀둔다. 콩나물은 머리와 꼬리를 떼어내고 다듬어서 데치고, 양상추와 양파는 채로 썰어 각각 찬물에 담갔다 물기를 빼둔다. 래디시는 얇게 썰어 준비하고, 무순은 뿌리를 자르고 흐르는 물에 씻어둔 다. 준비해둔 모든 재료를 먹기 좋게 그릇에 담고 소스와 함께 낸다.

Tteok Kalbi 떡갈비

The name, Tteok Kalbi, combines the names of two different Korean food items. "Tteok" is a Korean ricecake, and "Kalbi", is a type of marinated beef shortrib. Tteok Kalbi is a dish that utilizes a special method to make marinated beef shortribs as tender as ricecakes. Traditionally, Tteok Kalbi is made by removing the meat from the kalbi bones, grilling the bones separately, wrapping the grilled bones with coarsely chopped kalbi meat, and then cooking the meat and bones together. My mom wanted to have a little fun with this recipe, making a dish that plays a bit on the name. She simplified the procedure, making edible "bones" out of tteok, and using ground beef instead of chopped kalbi. It creates a dish that is true to the feeling of the original but is easier and more fun to eat.

33

Ingredients
• 1 pound ground beef • ½ pound rice cakes, cut into 2 inch long pieces
• 1 small onion, finely chopped • ½ of a carrot, finely chopped
• 1 tablespoon green onion, chopped • 1 teaspoon garlic, minced
• 2 tablespoons soy sauce • 1½ tablespoons brown sugar
• 1 tablespoon sesame oil • ¼ teaspoon black pepper
• 1 tablespoon cooking wine • Vegetable oil for greasing

Preheat oven to 400 F. Lightly grease a large baking dish with vegetable oil and set aside. Combine soy sauce, sesame seeds, black pepper, green onion, and minced garlic in a small bowl and set aside. Put ground beef, carrot and onion into a medium sized bowl. Stir together brown sugar and cooking wine until sugar is mostly dissolved. Pour sugar and wine mixture over the meat, carrot, and onion and mix until meat is well coated. Next, pour the soy sauce mixture over the meat and mix all of the ingredients for about 2 minutes. Then add sesame oil and mix again to coat.

Cook rice cakes in boiling water until soft. Remove from boiling water, rinse in cold water, and drain. Take a golf ball sized amount of the beef mixture, shape it into a rectangle, flatten it, and wrap the beef around a rice cake. Repeat, using the rest of the beef and rice cakes. Place the prepared tteok kalbi into the greased baking sheet and bake for about 20 minutes. Serve warm.

Alternately, you can make these tteok kalbi by cooking them in a frying pan.

Just heat a couple tablespoons of canola oil in a large frying pan over medium high heat, place into the hot pan, and cook for about 2 minutes on each side or until beef is fully cooked.

재료 • 다진 쇠고기 450g • 떡볶이 떡 225g, 2인치 길이로 썬다 • 작은 양파 1개, 곱게 다진다 • 당근 ½개, 곱게 다진다 • 다진 파 1큰술 • 다진 마늘 1작은술 • 간장 2큰술 • 흑설탕 1½큰술 • 참기름 1큰술 • 후추 ¼작은술 • 맛술 1큰술 그릇에 간장, 깨, 후추, 다진 파, 다진 마늘을 섞어둔다.

큰 그릇에 다진 재료들을 넣고 맛술과 흑설탕을 넣어 밑간을 한 후 섞어둔 양념을 부어 2분 정도 치댄다. 고루 섞이면 참기름을 넣어 다시 한 번 섞는다. 떡을 끓는 물에 살짝 데쳐 물렁해지면 찬물에 식혀놓고, 양념해둔 고기를 골프공 크기로 떼어 얇게 펴서 떡을 말아준다. 200도로 예열해둔 오븐에 넣어 20분간 구워내거나 기름을 두른 달군 팬에 약 2분씩 뒤집어가며 익혀낸다.

Oxtail Jjim 쇠꼬리찜

My mom loves oxtail, but in Korea it tends to be expensive, so she was not able to cook with it very often. In the United States, it is much more affordable, so my mother is constantly cooking different dishes with oxtail. Making Oxtail Jjim is one of her favorite recipes to make with oxtail because it makes the soup extremely thick and rich. It turns an already decadent preparation into something truly indulgent.

Ingredients

- 3 ⅓ pounds of beef oxtail
- ½ of a daikon radish, diced into 1 inch pieces with edges rounded and cooked
  (They should look somewhat like small, peeled potatoes.)
- 2 carrots, diced into 1 inch pieces with edges rounded and cooked
- 10 cooked chestnuts can be replaced with 1 peeled and diced potato
- 5 dried Asian dates • 3 dried shitake mushrooms, soaked to reconstitute, quartered
- 2 slices of peeled ginger • 10 whole black peppercorns
- 2 tablespoons green onion, chopped (for garnish)

Ingredients for Marinade

- 10 tablespoons soy sauce • 5 tablespoons lightly packed brown sugar
- 4 tablespoons green onion, chopped • 2 tablespoons garlic, minced
- 2 tablespoons toasted sesame seeds • 2 tablespoons sesame oil
- 2 teaspoons ground black pepper • 3 tablespoons mirin

Mix together all ingredients for marinade in a bowl and set aside.

Rinse oxtail well in cold water and allow the blood to soak out for at least 1 hour. Trim any excess fat off. Take a knife and make three or four cuts into the meat.

In a 5-quart saucepan, combine 8 cups of cold water, ginger and peppercorns and bring to a boil. Add the oxtail and continue to boil until it is tender, about an hour. Occasionally skim the oil from the surface of the boiling liquid.

After the meat becomes tender, remove the oxtails from the pot and reserve the cooking broth in a separate container. Put the oxtails back into the pot and pour the marinating sauce over the oxtails, mixing to coat thoroughly. Let sit for about 30 minutes. Add 2 cups of the reserved broth, daikon radish, carrot, and shitake mushrooms to the pot and bring to a boil. Then lower the heat and simmer until vegetables are tender, about 30 minutes. In the last few minutes of cooking, add chestnuts and dates, and return to a boil. Remove from heat, garnish with chopped green onion, and serve hot.

재료 • 쇠꼬리 3.3파운드(1.5kg) • 무 ½개, 사방 1인치 크기로 잘라 둥글게 깎아 데쳐둔다 • 당근 2개, 무와 같은 크기로 깎아 데친다 • 밤 10개, 껍질을 벗기고 익힌다 • 대추 5개 • 불린 표고버섯 3개, 4등분한다 • 생강 2쪽 • 통후추 10알 • 다진 파 2큰술(장식용) 쇠꼬리 양념장 재료 • 간장 10큰술 • 흑설탕 5큰술 • 다진 파 4큰술 • 다진 마늘 2큰술 • 볶은 깨 2큰술 • 참기름 2큰술 • 후추 2작은술 • 맛술 3큰술

쇠꼬리를 찬물에 깨끗이 씻어 1시간 정도 담가 핏물을 뺀 후 기름을 떼어내고 돌아가며 서너 군데 칼집을 넣는다. 끓는 물에 쇠꼬리와 생강, 통후추를 넣고 거품을 걷어내며 1시간 정도 푹 삶는다. 쇠꼬리는 건져 준비한 양념장을 고루 끼얹어 간이 배도록 30분 정도 두고, 국물은 깨끗하게 걸러 기름을 제거해둔다. 냄비에 양념해둔 쇠꼬리를 넣고 기름을 걷어낸 쇠꼬리 삶았던 물을 2컵 정도 자작하게 부은 후, 깎아놓은 무, 당근, 표고버섯을 넣고 약한 불에 한소끔 끓인다. 쇠꼬리와 채소가 푹 익으면 밤과 대추를 넣어 다시 한 번 끓여 뜨겁게 낸다.

Shabu Shabu 샤부샤부

Shabu Shabu is a type of food preparation. You cook thinly sliced meat, seafood, or vegetables in a hot pot of boiling broth by dipping each item with a "swishing" motion in the hot broth. The name "Shabu Shabu" comes from this swishing action. The broth is typically served at the table in an electric or gas powered hot pot. At Shabu Shabu restaurants, the hot pot is often embedded at the center of each table with a dial to adjust the heat level. If you do not own an electric hot pot, you can boil the broth at the stove and then set it over an alcohol burner, similar to those used by catering companies to keep dishes hot. It is important that the broth stay hot enough to cook the various ingredients, so be sure to keep the broth at a simmer.

Ingredients for Shabu Shabu

- 1 ½ pounds beef loin or ribeye, very thinly sliced
- 1 bundle enoki mushrooms, ends trimmed
- 3 dried shitake mushrooms, soaked in warm water
  to reconstitute for 30 minutes, stems discarded and cut into strips
- ½ red bell pepper, cut into very thin strips
- 1 package konjac, cut into bite size pieces (optional)
- 4 bunches baby bok choy, washed, stalks
  and leaves separated, and cut diagonally

Ingredients for Broth

- 8 cups water • 5 inch square of kombu
- 1 inch thick slice of daikon radish • ½ cup bonito flakes
- 1 teaspoon soy sauce • 1 teaspoon salt

Ingredients for Sesame Dipping Sauce

- 4 tablespoons dashi broth • 1 tablespoon mirin
- 1 tablespoon peanut butter • 2 tablespoons soy sauce
- 1 tablespoon vinegar • 3 tablespoons toasted sesame seeds, ground
- 1 tablespoon onion, grated

Ingredients for Ponze Dipping Sauce

- 3 tablespoons daikon radish juice • 1 tablespoon mirin
- 2 tablespoons lemon juice • 2 tablespoons soy sauce
- 2 teaspoons sugar

Ingredients for Soy Dipping Sauce

- 3 tablespoons basic sauce
  (Basic sauce is made of 5 parts vinegar to 4 parts sugar to 1 part salt.)
- 4 tablespoons dashi broth or chicken stock
- 2 tablespoons soy sauce
- 1 teaspoon prepared Asian hot mustard
- 1 tablespoon toasted sesame seeds
- 1 tablespoon green onion, chopped

Mix together the ingredients for each separate dipping sauce and set aside.

Place the 8 cups of water in a large saucepan. Wipe down kombu with a damp paper towel and soak it in the water for about 10 minutes. Add daikon radish and soy sauce, bring to a boil, and then turn off the heat. Add bonito flakes and leave for 15 minutes. Strain the liquid and return to the pot. Add salt and bring liquid to a boil.

Arrange the other ingredients for the shabu shabu on a large plate. Set an electric hot pot at the table and add the boiling broth. Place bowls with each dipping sauce at the table. To begin eating, place a slice of beef into the boiling broth and swish it back and forth until it is fully cooked. Dip the cooked meat into a dipping sauce of your choice, combining more than one sauce if you wish. Continue to cook the rest of the ingredients, eating as you go. Skim off any foam or fat that rises to the surface of the broth as you continue cooking. Makes four servings.

재료(4인분) • 쇠고기 등심 680g(1.5 파운드), 샤부샤부용으로 아주 얇게 썬다 • 팽이버섯 1봉지, 끝을 잘라내고 다듬는다 • 마른 표고버섯 3개, 30분 정도 미지근한 물에 불려서 기둥을 떼고 채 썬다 • 홍피망 ½개, 채 썬다 • 곤약 1봉지, 먹기 좋은 크기로 썰어 꼬아둔다 • 청경채 4송이, 줄기를 떼어서 씻은 후 어슷하게 썰어둔다 육수 재료 • 물 8컵 • 다시마(사방 10cm) 1장 • 무 1인치 한 토막 • 가쓰오부시 ½컵 • 간장 1작은술 • 소금 1작은술 소스 재료 [깨 소스] • 다시 국물 4큰술 • 맛술 1큰술 • 땅콩버터 1큰술 • 간장 2큰술 • 식초 1큰술 • 깨소금 3큰술 • 간 양파 1큰술 [폰즈 소스] • 무즙 3큰술 • 맛술 1큰술 • 레몬즙(유자즙) 2큰술 • 간장 2큰술 • 설탕 2작은술 [간장 소스] • 베이식 소스 3큰술(식초5 : 설탕4 : 소금1) • 다시 국물(또는 닭육수) 4큰술 • 간장 2큰술 • 갠 겨자 1작은술 • 볶은 깨 1큰술 • 다진 파 1큰술

소스 재료를 각각 섞어 소스를 만들어둔다. 다시마를 젖은 수건으로 닦아 물 8컵과 함께 큰 냄비에 넣고 10분간 두었다가 무와 간장을 넣고 불에 올린다. 물이 끓어오르면 불을 끄고 가쓰오부시를 넣어 15분 정도 두었다 걸러낸다. 소금으로 간을 해서 냄비에 다시 넣고 약한 불에 끓인다. 큰 접시에 준비한 재료들을 예쁘게 둘러 담고 원하는 소스도 준비한다. 테이블에 전기팬을 놓고 국물을 넣어 끓이면서 원하는 재료들을 넣어 살랑살랑 흔들어 익혀서 소스에 찍어 먹는다.

Korean Steak Kabobs 한국식 스테이크 꼬치구이

Kabobs are the easiest way to make a meal in the summer, when spending time over a hot stove is the last thing you want to do. You can marinate these ahead of time, refrigerate, and grill them right before it is time to eat. As you can add any number of vegetables and proteins, kabobs are very versatile. They make good appetizers or even a full meal along with a side dish or two.

Ingredients

• 2 pounds beef sirloin or ribeye, cut into 1 ½ inch cubes
• 1 medium onion, cut into 1 ½ inch squares • 1 green bell pepper, cut into 1 ½ inch squares
• 1 red bell pepper, cut into 1 ½ inch squares • 1 orange bell pepper, cut into 1 ½ inch squares
• 1 zucchini, cut into 1 ½ inch squares • Salt and pepper
• Bamboo skewers, soaked in cold water for 30 minutes

Ingredients for Marinade

• 4 tablespoons soy sauce • 1 tablespoon brown sugar • 1 tablespoon rice wine
• 3 tablespoons canola oil • 1 tablespoon sesame oil • 1 teaspoon chopped ginger
• 2 teaspoons minced garlic • 1 tablespoon chopped green onion
• ¼ teaspoon ground black pepper

Combine ingredients for marinade, mix thoroughly, and set aside. Place sirloin in a large bowl and season with salt and pepper. Pour in half of the marinade, tossing to coat. Cover and refrigerate for a couple of hours to allow the flavors to meld. In a separate bowl, add vegetables and season with salt and pepper. Pour in the other half of the marinade and toss well. Cover and set aside.

Assemble the kabobs by alternating steak and vegetables on the bamboo skewers. Preheat the grill, keeping track of where the hottest places on the grill are. If you have a larger gas grill with temperature controls, heat one side on high heat and the other on low heat. Place the skewers on the hottest part of the grill, or on the side that is on high. Cover and cook for five minutes. Flip the kabobs, cover, and grill for another five minutes. Move the kabobs to the side on low heat or a cooler part of the grill and cook for about three more minutes. Makes four servings.

재료(4인분) • 쇠고기 등심 또는 채끝살 900g(2파운드), 사방 1.5인치 크기로 썬다 • 양파 1개, 사방 1.5인치 크기로 썬다 • 청피망 1개, 사방 1.5인치 크기로 썬다 • 홍피망 1개, 사방 1.5인치 크기로 썬다 • 오렌지색 피망 1개, 사방 1.5인치 크기로 썬다 • 호박 1개, 피망과 같은 크기로 썬다 • 소금, 후추 약간 • 꼬치, 30분 정도 물에 담가둔다 재는 양념 • 간장 4큰술 • 흑설탕 1큰술 • 청주 1큰술 • 카놀라유 3큰술 • 참기름 1큰술 • 다진 생강 1작은술 • 다진 마늘 2작은술 • 다진 파 1큰술 • 후추 ¼작은술 재료들을 잘 섞어놓는다.

큰 그릇에 고기를 넣어 소금과 후추로 밑간을 하고 만들어둔 양념의 반을 넣어 잘 섞어 냉장고에서 2시간가량 재워둔다. 다른 그릇에 썰어놓은 채소들을 넣고 나머지 양념장을 부어 잘 섞어 재워놓는다. 그릴을 한쪽은 불이 세게, 한쪽은 불이 약하게 달구어둔다. 물에 담가두었던 꼬치를 꺼내 물기를 닦고 고기와 채소들을 색을 맞춰 번갈아 가며 끼워준다. 센 불에 5분 정도 그릴 뚜껑을 덮고 구운 후 뒤집어서 다시 5분간 구운 후 약불로 옮겨 3분 정도 구워낸다.

chicken

Lemon Miso
Chicken Salad 레몬 미소 치킨샐러드

Tired of the typical chicken salads, my mom decided to come up with a new version using Japanese flavors. This salad is a fresh new twist on a classic.

Ingredients

• ¾ pound chicken breast fillets • 1 tablespoon mirin
• 1 tablespoon vegetable oil plus more for cooking
• Salt and pepper • 2 cups spring mix or any salad green
• 1 red radish, thinly sliced

Ingredients for Dressing

• 2 tablespoons white miso(Saikyo miso)
• 1 teaspoon toasted sesame seeds • 1 tablespoon rice vinegar
• 1 tablespoon sesame oil • 1 tablespoon mirin
• 1 tablespoon lemon juice • pinch of salt

Combine all of the ingredients for the dressing, mixing until thoroughly combined. Set aside.

Place chicken into a large bowl and pour the mirin, salt, pepper, and vegetable oil over the meat, flipping to coat both sides. Marinate for 10 minutes. Heat vegetable oil in a large frying pan over medium high heat. Add the chicken and cook until the meat is fully done. The chicken should be opaque and cut into one inch pieces and set aside.

Arrange chicken on a bed of salad greens add the sliced radishes. Add lemon miso dressing to taste. Makes two servings.

재료(2인분) • 닭가슴살 350g(¾파운드) • 맛술 1큰술 • 식용유 1큰술 • 소금, 후추 약간 • 샐러드용 상추 또는 스프링믹스 2컵, 씻어서 물기를 빼둔다 • 래디시 1개, 얇게 썬다 레몬 미소 드레싱 재료 • 시로미소(사이쿄미소) 2큰술 • 볶은 깨 1작은술 • 식초 1큰술 • 참기름 1큰술 • 맛술 1큰술 • 레몬즙 1큰술 • 소금 약간 드레싱 재료를 잘 섞어둔다.

닭가슴살을 맛술과 소금, 후추, 식용유로 밑간하여 10분간 둔다. 달군 프라이팬에 밑간해둔 닭가슴살을 지져서 잘 익힌 다음 접시에 옮겨 식혀서 먹기 좋은 크기로 썬다. 준비해둔 스프링믹스와 래디시를 접시에 깔고 그 위에 닭가슴살을 올린 다음 드레싱을 끼얹어낸다.

Chicken Lettuce Wraps 닭고기 양상추 쌈

One of the great things about this recipe, other than how delicious it is, is that it is very versatile. I have used the methods and flavorings in this recipe to make a dish of pork and green beans, which was a big hit at my house for dinner. These lettuce wraps make a great lunch or a light dinner.

Ingredients

- ⅓ pound chicken breast, cut into ½ inch cubes • ½ small red onion, chopped
- 10 leaves iceberg lettuce or boston lettuce • ½ carrot, peeled and shredded
- 2 dried shitake mushrooms, soaked in the warm water to reconstitute
  for 30 minutes, stems removed and cut into small cubes
- ½ red bell pepper, cut into small cubes
- 2 ounces of mung bean noodles, cut into 2 inch lengths
- 2 cloves garlic, thinly sliced • ½ inch piece fresh ginger, thinly sliced
- ½ tablespoon black bean paste • canola oil for frying

Ingredients for Marinade

- 1 tablespoon soy sauce • 1 tablespoon mirin
- 1 tablespoon cornstarch • ⅛ teaspoon black pepper

Heat canola oil in a deep frying pan over high heat and fry mung bean noodles until crisp. Drain well on a paper towel. Marinate chicken with soy sauce, mirin, cornstarch and black pepper and set aside. Heat canola oil in a large frying pan over medium high heat. Add sliced garlic and ginger and cook until light brown. Remove from pan and discard. Add chicken and cook until the pieces are not quite cooked through, about three minutes. Then add chopped onion, red pepper, and mushrooms. Cook vegetables until tender but still crisp. Add black bean paste to the chicken and vegetable mixture and combine well.

Scoop portions of the chicken and vegetables onto lettuce leaves and garnish with fried mung bean noodles and shredded carrots. Makes two servings.

재료(2인분) • 닭가슴살 150g(⅓ 파운드), 1센티 크기로 썬다 • 붉은 양파 ½개, 1센티 크기로 썬다 • 양상추 또는 보스톤 상추 10잎, 쌈 싸기 좋은 크기로 잘라 찬물에 담갔다 물기를 빼둔다 • 당근 ½개, 껍질을 벗기고 채 썬다 • 마른 표고버섯 2장, 미지근한 물에 30분 정도 불려서 기둥을 떼고 잘게 썬다 • 홍피망 ½개, 1센티 크기로 썬다 • 당면 2온스, 5센티 길이로 잘라둔다 • 마늘 2개, 얇게 편으로 썬다 • 생강 1조각(1센티 크기), 얇게 편으로 썬다 • 춘장 ½큰술 • 카놀라유 밑간 양념 재료 • 간장 1큰술 • 맛술 1큰술 • 전분 1큰술 • 후추 ⅛작은술

프라이팬에 카놀라유를 넣고 뜨거워지면 당면을 넣어 파삭하게 튀겨내어 종이타월에 기름을 빼놓는다. 닭고기를 밑간 양념에 재워두고, 중간 불로 팬을 달구어 기름을 두르고 마늘, 생강을 넣어 갈색이 될 때까지 두었다가 마늘과 생강은 꺼내고 밑간해둔 닭고기를 넣어 볶는다. 닭고기가 반 정도 익으면 나머지 재료들을 넣어 같이 볶아준 후 춘장으로 간을 한다. 준비한 상추 위에 고기 채소 볶음을 놓고 튀긴 당면과 채 썬 당근을 얹어낸다.

Spicy Chicken Curry 매운 닭고기 카레

My mom developed this recipe because she began to dislike eating curry, a dish she has enjoyed since she was a child. When she stopped to analyze this change, she realized that the difference between the curry she ate now and the curry of her youth, is that curry is not often made from scratch anymore. Premade blocks of curry take away the variety and subtlety of seasoning that comes with making curry from scratch. This recipe is the return to the curry of my mom's youth, and of course, her love of a favorite dish.

Ingredients
• ½ pound chicken breasts or thighs, fat removed and thinly sliced
• 2 small onions, julienned • I medium apple, peeled and thinly sliced
• 2 green chilies, seeded and thinly sliced • I cup green beans, diagonally sliced
• 4 cups hot chicken stock • ½ teaspoon salt • ¼ teaspoon pepper
• I clove garlic, chopped • I teaspoon chopped ginger • I tablespoon olive oil

Ingredients for Curry Roux
• I tablespoon butter • I tablespoon canola oil • 3 tablespoons flour
• I ½ to 2 tablespoons Japanese curry powder

Heat olive oil in a heavy bottomed pot over medium heat. Add chicken and onion and cook for 5 minutes. Add ginger and garlic and cook for few more minutes, until fragrant. Add chicken stock and apple and bring to a boil. Lower the heat and simmer for one hour. Add salt and pepper to taste. Blanch the green beans in a pot of boiling water until tender, then drain.

In a small frying pan melt the butter and canola oil over medium heat until any foaming subsides.

Add the flour, and cook the mixture over medium-low heat, stirring constantly, until light brown in color.

Remove the pan from the heat, add the curry powder, mix well and set aside. Add curry mixture to chicken stock with the cooked green beans and sliced green chilies. Simmer for 10 more minutes. Serve curry on a bed of cooked rice.

재료 • 닭가슴살 또는 닭다릿살 250g(½파운드), 껍질과 기름을 제거하고 얇게 저민다 • 작은 양파 2개, 채 썬다 • 사과 1개, 껍질과 씨를 제거하고 얇게 썬다 • 매운 청고추 2개, 씨를 빼고 얇게 썬다 • 그린빈 1컵, 길게 어슷하게 썬다 • 닭육수 4컵 • 소금 ½작은술 • 후추 ¼작은술 • 마늘 1개, 다진다 • 다진 생강 1작은술 • 올리브유 1큰술 카레 페이스트 재료 • 버터 1큰술 + 카놀라유 1큰술 • 밀가루 3큰술 • 카레가루 1 ½ 또는 2큰술

두꺼운 냄비를 중간 불로 달구어 기름을 두르고 양파와 닭고기를 넣어 5분간 익힌 다음 생강과 마늘을 넣어 볶아 향을 낸다. 거기에 닭육수와 준비해둔 사과를 넣어 끓기 시작하면 불을 줄여 1시간 정도 더 끓인 후 소금, 후추로 간한다. 끓는 물에 준비해둔 그린빈을 데쳐내어 물기를 빼둔다. 작은 팬을 달구어 기름과 버터를 넣고 버터가 다 녹으면 밀가루를 넣어 옅은 갈색이 될 때까지 저어준다. 갈색이 되면 불에서 내려 카레가루를 넣어 잘 섞어 카레 페이스트를 만들어둔다. 냄비 안의 국물이 반 정도로 줄면 준비해둔 카레 페이스트와 그린빈, 청고추를 넣어 약한 불에 10분 정도 더 끓인 후 밥 위에 부어낸다.

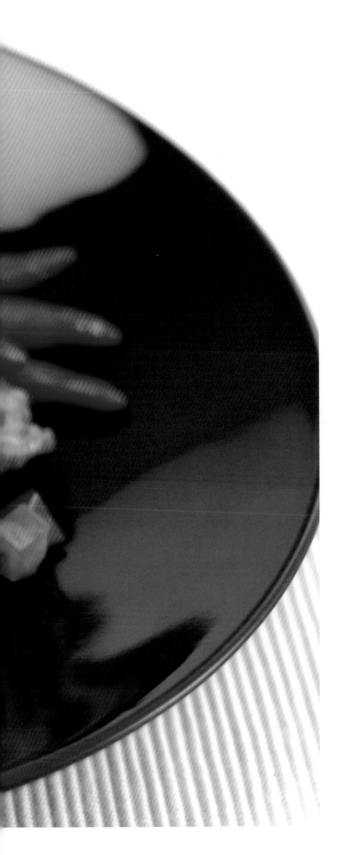

Kanpoonggi 깐풍기

I went to college about thirty minutes outside a large city and while it was filled with great restaurants, the surrounding suburbs had a few favorites that were frequently visited by the students on my campus. One such restaurant was a place that made the best kanpoonggi I have ever tasted. My friends and I would get several orders and just sit there eating until all of the spicy, salty, sweet chicken was reduced to a pile of bones. Every time I bit into that crispy chicken, I couldn't imagine tasting anything better. This recipe for kanpoonggi takes me right back to my college days, and allows me to bring that memory right into my own kitchen.

Ingredients

- 4 chicken thighs (1 pound) • 1 tablespoon cooking wine • 1 tablespoon ginger juice
- ¼ teaspoon salt • ⅛ teaspoon black pepper • 1 egg
- 6 tablespoons cornstarch + 6 tablespoons water • ¼ red bell pepper, diced
- 2 chili peppers, sliced thinly • ¼ red onion, diced • canola oil

Ingredients for Sauce

- 1 tablespoon chopped ginger • 1 tablespoon chopped garlic • 1 tablespoon cooking wine
- 1 tablespoon sugar • 2 tablespoons soy sauce • ¼ teaspoon black pepper
- 1 tablespoon sesame oil • canola oil for frying

Cut the chicken into bite sized pieces. Mix egg, cooking wine, ginger juice, salt and black pepper. Place chicken in a medium sized bowl and pour egg mixture over the pieces, mixing to coat thoroughly. Marinate chicken for several minutes. In a small bowl, dissolve the cornstarch in the 6 tablespoons of water and set aside. After about 10 minutes, the cornstarch should separate from the water. Pour off the water, leaving the cornstarch residue behind.

Heat canola oil in a large, deep skillet over high heat. The oil should be about one inch in depth. Dip the marinated chicken cubes into the cornstarch mixture. Deep fry the chicken until it is golden brown and crispy (about 6 minutes), and remove from the oil. Fry a second time, being careful not to burn the chicken.

In a separate wok heat 2 tablespoons of the canola oil and sauté garlic and ginger until fragrant. Add soy sauce, sugar, cooking wine, and boil for several seconds. Add fried chicken and prepared vegetables and cook for a few more minutes. Add sesame oil and black pepper, mix well and serve.

재료 • 닭다릿살 4쪽(450g) • 맛술 1큰술 • 생강즙 1큰술 • 소금 ¼작은술 • 후추 ⅛작은술 • 달걀 1개 • 전분 6큰술 + 물 6큰술 • 홍피망 ¼개, 잘게 썬다 • 매운 청고추 2개, 잘게 썬다 • 붉은 양파 ¼개, 잘게 썬다 • 카놀라유 소스 재료 • 다진 생강 1큰술 • 다진 마늘 1큰술 • 맛술 1큰술 • 설탕 1큰술 • 간장 2큰술 • 후추 ¼작은술 • 참기름 1큰술 • 카놀라유(튀김용)

닭다릿살을 먹기 좋은 크기로 자르고, 달걀, 맛술, 생강즙, 소금, 후추를 섞어 닭고기에 넣어 재워둔다. 작은 그릇에 녹말과 같은 양의 물을 넣고 잘 섞어 10분간 놓아두었다가 앙금이 가라앉으면 물은 버리고 재워둔 닭고기에 앙금을 넣어 버무린다. 두꺼운 팬에 기름을 1인치 정도 깊이로 넣고 뜨거워지면 닭고기를 넣어 바삭하게 두 번 튀겨낸다. 다른 팬을 달궈 카놀라유를 2큰술 두르고 다져놓은 마늘과 생강을 볶아 향을 내고 간장, 설탕, 맛술을 넣고 살짝 끓여준다. 소스에 썰어놓은 채소와 튀긴 닭고기를 넣고 살짝 볶은 후 마지막으로 참기름과 후추를 넣어 잘 섞어 접시에 담아낸다.

tip 1. 고기나 생선을 튀기기 전에 생강을 한 조각 넣어주면 고기의 잡내를 잡을 수 있습니다. 2. 생강을 토막 내어 얼려두었다가 필요할 때마다 한 조각씩 꺼내어 전자레인지에 30초 정도 돌려 짜면 쉽게 생강즙을 만들 수 있어요. 3. 생강즙을 짜낸 조각은 버리지 마시고 튀김할 때 사용하세요. 4. 고기에 불린 녹말을 입힐 때는 얇게 입혀야 맛이 더 좋아요.

Butter Fried Drunken Chicken 술에 재워 버터에 지진 닭고기

I am always looking for new ways to cook chicken, and this is recipe is both easy and flavorful. Although the name implies fatty deliciousness, the whole recipe only uses one tablespoon of butter, which is a pretty small price to pay for such a great meal.

Ingredients

• 2 boneless, skinless, chicken breasts, cut into 2 inch pieces
• 2 boneless, skinless, chicken thighs, cut into 2 inch pieces
• I tablespoon butter • I tablespoon olive oil
• ¼ cup rice wine • ¼ teaspoon sea salt
• ⅛ teaspoon freshly ground pepper • I tablespoon ginger juice
• 2 cloves garlic, thinly sliced • I tablespoon green onion, chopped
• 3 baby bok choy, separated and steamed • I cup green cabbage, shredded
• 2 king trumpet mushrooms, shredded (optional)

Season the chicken with rice wine, ginger juice, salt and black pepper and set aside.

Melt butter in a large heavy skillet. Add olive oil and sauté seasoned chicken until golden brown on one side. Turn the chicken over, add mushrooms if you wish, and cover. Cook for one more minute.

Remove chicken and vegetables to a serving plate, being sure to get all of the pan juices. Garnish with steamed bok choy and shredded cabbage. Serve with cooked rice or steamed buns.

재료 • 닭가슴살 2개, 2인치 크기로 먹기 좋게 자른다 • 닭다릿살 2개, 2인치 크기로 먹기 좋게 자른다 • 버터 1큰술 • 올리브유 1큰술 • 청주 ¼컵 • 바다소금 ¼작은술 • 후추 ⅛작은술 • 생강즙 1큰술 • 마늘 2개, 얇게 편으로 썬다 • 다진 파 1큰술 • 청경채 3개, 밑동을 자르고 뜯어서 파랗게 데친다 • 채 썬 양배추 1컵 • (선택) 새송이버섯 2개, 채 썬다

닭고기에 정종, 생강즙, 소금, 후추로 밑간을 해둔다. 달군 팬에 버터를 녹인 다음 올리브유를 넣고 썰어 둔 마늘을 넣어 볶아 향을 낸 후 밑간해둔 닭고기를 넣어 한 면이 노릇해질 때까지 지져서 뒤집은 다음 썰어놓은 버섯을 넣고 뚜껑을 덮어 1분 정도 더 익힌다. 닭고기와 버섯이 익으면 접시에 준비해둔 청경채와 양배추를 곁들여 함께 담아낸다. 밥이나 꽃빵과 같이 먹는다.

Teriyaki Chicken Thighs 닭고기 데리야키

Like so many other recipes in this collection, the flavors in this recipe are infinitely adaptable. The teriyaki sauce can be used with many different kinds of protein. I have had great success adapting this recipe for salmon fillets, strips of thinly sliced beef, and even tofu. For the vegetable component of this dish, I like to check out what is seasonal and fresh at the farmer's market and use that. Broccoli, bell peppers, onions, and cabbage all work beautifully. *Cook's Note: The chicken can also be cooked on a grill. Just brush teriyaki sauce over chicken while as it cooks, much like a barbeque sauce.

Ingredients
- 2 pounds boneless, skinless, chicken thigh meat • 1 tablespoon rice wine
- ⅛ teaspoon black pepper • 2 tablespoons vegetable oil
- 6 asparagus, tough ends snapped off, steamed and cut in half vertically
- 6 white asparagus, tough ends snapped off, steamed and cut in half vertically (optional)
- 4 tablespoons teriyaki sauce (recipe below)
- 1 tablespoon green onion, chopped (for garnish) • 4 cups cooked rice

Place chicken in a large bowl and season with rice wine and black pepper. Heat the vegetable oil in a large frying pan over medium high heat and cook both sides of the chicken until well browned. Add teriyaki sauce and continue to cook until the chicken is done. Add steamed asparagus and cook until warmed through, about one minute. Garnish with chopped green onion, and serve hot with or without cooked rice. Makes four servings.

Ingredients for Teriyaki Sauce
- ¼ cup soy sauce • ¼ cup mirin • ¼ cup chicken stock or water
- 2 teaspoons fresh ginger, grated • 3 tablespoons brown sugar
- 1 teaspoon garlic, minced • 1 teaspoon cornstarch + 1 tablespoon cold water

Combine chicken stock or water, soy sauce, brown sugar, mirin, garlic and ginger in a saucepan and bring to a boil, stirring constantly. Dissolve cornstarch in ¼ cup of cold water and add to sauce. Stir constantly until the sauce thickens. If the sauce is too thick add a little water to thin it out.

재료(4인분) • 닭다릿살 2파운드(900g) • 청주 1큰술 • 후추 ⅛작은술 • 식용유 2큰술 • 데리야키 소스 4큰술 • 다진 파 1큰술(장식용) • 밥 4공기 • (선택) 아스파라거스 6개, 끝을 다듬고 데쳐서 길게 반 가른다 • (선택) 흰색 아스파라거스 6개, 끝을 다듬고 데쳐서 길게 반 가른다

닭고기에 청주를 넣어 밑간을 해둔다. 큰 프라이팬을 달구어 기름을 두르고 밑간해둔 닭고기를 넣어 노릇해질 때까지 앞뒤로 지진 다음 데리야키 소스를 부어 닭고기가 속까지 다 익을 때까지 구워준다. 접시에 준비해둔 아스파라거스를 깔고 그 위에 데리야키 치킨을 올린다. 밥을 곁들여내도 좋다.

tip 닭고기를 먼저 그릴에 구워 어느 정도 익으면 데리야키 소스를 발라 다 익을 때까지 구워내도 좋다.

데리야키 소스 재료 • 간장 ¼컵 • 맛술 ¼컵 • 닭육수 또는 물 ¼컵 • 다진 생강 2작은술 • 흑설탕 3큰술 • 다진 마늘 1작은술 • 전분 1작은술 + 물 1큰술. 잘 섞어둔다

그릇에 물과 전분을 넣어 잘 섞어둔다. 냄비에 간장, 닭육수, 맛술, 흑설탕, 다진 마늘, 다진 생강을 넣고 저으면서 끓인다. 끓기 시작하면 풀어놓은 전분을 넣어 농도를 조절한다.

Spicy Chicken with Vegetables 매운 닭갈비

The recipe takes a dish most often served at bars and elevates it. It is spicy, comforting and perfect alongside a cold glass of beer. While you could substitute chicken breast for the chicken leg meat, using dark meat ensures that this dish has plenty of flavor. *Cook's Note: This dish tastes best served immediately, while it is piping hot.

Ingredients

• 2 pounds chicken leg meat, cut into 1 inch pieces
• 1 carrot, peeled and cut into round slices
• 1 small onion, cut into ½ inch strips • 2 leaves red cabbage, cut into ½ inch strips
• 1 green pepper, cut into bite sized pieces • 1 tablespoon toasted sesame seeds
• 3 tablespoons canola oil • ½ cup chicken broth

Ingredients for Marinade

• 2 tablespoons mirin • 2 tablespoons soy sauce
• 3 tablespoons Korean hot pepper paste (gochujang) • 2 tablespoons brown sugar
• 2 tablespoons water • 1 teaspoon garlic, minced
• 1 tablespoon chopped green onion • ¼ teaspoon black pepper
• 1 tablespoon toasted sesame seeds • 2 tablespoons sesame oil

Combine Korean hot pepper paste, soy sauce, mirin, sesame seeds, black pepper, green onion and minced garlic in a small bowl and set aside. This is the marinade for the chicken. Stir together brown sugar and water until sugar is mostly dissolved. Pour sugar water mixture over the chicken and mix until it is well coated. Let sit for about five minutes. Pour prepared marinade over the meat and combine. Then add sesame oil and mix again to coat. Let meat marinate for 30 minutes, or if you wish, you can marinate it overnight.

Heat two tablespoons of canola oil in a large frying pan over high heat. Add vegetables and cook until slightly softened, about two minutes. Remove the vegetables from the frying pan and set aside. Return the pan to the stove. Add an additional tablespoon of canola oil to the pan. When the pan is hot, add marinated chicken. Continue to cook the chicken for about three more minutes, then add chicken broth and simmer until chicken is fully cooked. Add the vegetables back into the pan and cook for one additional minute. Garnish with sesame seeds and serve hot. Makes four servings.

재료 • 닭다릿살 2파운드(900g), 1인치 크기로 썬다 • 당근 1개, 껍질을 벗기고 둥글고 얇게 썬다. • 양파 1개, 0.5인치 정도로 굵게 채 썬다 • 적양배추 2장, 먹기 좋은 크기로 썬다 • 청피망 1개, 먹기 좋은 크기로 썬다 • 볶은 깨 1큰술 • 카놀라유 3큰술 • 닭육수 ½컵 닭고기 양념장 재료 • 맛술 2큰술 • 간장 2큰술 • 고추장 3큰술 • 흑설탕 2큰술 • 물 2큰술 • 다진 마늘 1작은술 • 다진 파 1큰술 • 후추 ¼작은술 • 볶은 깨 1작은술 • 참기름 2큰술

작은 그릇에 고추장, 간장, 맛술, 볶은 깨, 마늘, 파, 후추를 섞어둔다. 흑설탕과 물을 섞어 설탕이 녹으면 먹기 좋은 크기로 잘라 놓은 닭고기에 넣어 밑간을 하여 5분간 둔다. 밑간해둔 닭고기에 양념장을 넣어 무쳐놓고 참기름을 넣어 다시 한 번 잘 섞어 30분 정도 두거나 냉장고에 넣어 하룻밤 둔다. 달군 팬에 기름을 2큰술 두르고 썰어둔 채소를 넣어 색이 살도록 살짝 볶아내고 다시 팬을 불에 올려 달군 후 나머지 기름을 넣고 재워둔 닭고기를 넣어 3분 정도 볶아준다. 고기가 어느 정도 익으면 준비해둔 닭육수를 넣어 볶는다. 고기가 다 익으면 익힌 채소를 넣고 다시 1분 정도 더 볶아 접시에 담고 볶은 깨로 장식해낸다.

noo dles

& rice

California Rolls 캘리포니아롤

With all her cooking experience, it is rare that my mother gets truly excited about a new cooking technique or recipe. The method for seasoning sushi rice in this recipe is one of those discoveries that had her urging me to get into the kitchen so I could try it for myself. Adding lemon juice to the sushi rice complements the tartness of the rice vinegar, but also adds brightness from the citrus and more depth of flavor. It's a small twist that adds a big difference in the flavor of the rolls.

Ingredients
• 1 avocado, peeled, pitted and sliced into ¼-½ inch strips
• ½ English (hothouse) cucumber, peeled and cut into thin strips 8 inches long
• 10 crab sticks • 2 tablespoons sesame seeds, toasted
• 2 tablespoons flying fish roe • Pickled ginger, for serving
• Wasabi paste, for serving • Soy sauce, for serving
• 1 package (10 sheets) of nori (seaweed) • 1 recipe sushi rice

Cover a bamboo rolling mat with plastic wrap. Cut nori sheets in 8x6 pieces. Lay 1 sheet of nori, shiny side down, on the plastic covered mat. Wet your fingers with water and spread about ½ cup of the rice evenly onto the nori. Sprinkle the rice with sesame seeds. Turn the sheet of nori over so that the rice side is down on top of the bamboo mat. Place cucumber strips, avocado and crab in the center of the sheet. Remember, the nori and rice will have to roll around the fillings, so be careful how much of each ingredient you place on the sheet.

Grab the edge of the mat closest to you, keeping the fillings in place with your fingers, and roll it into a tight cylinder, using the mat to shape the cylinder. Pull away the mat and set aside. Re-cover with clean plastic wrap. Repeat until all of the rice has been used. Cut each roll into 8 pieces. Garnish the outside of the rolls with flying fish roe.

Serve with pickled ginger, wasabi and soy sauce.

재료 • 아보카도 1개, 씨와 껍질을 제거하고 0.25~0.5인치 길이로 가늘게 썬다 • 오이 ½개, 껍질을 벗기고 8인치 길이로 가늘게 썬다 • 게살 10개 • 붉은 깨 2큰술 • 날치 알 2큰술 • 절인 생강 • 와사비 • 간장 • 김 10장 • 초밥 5공기

김발을 지퍼백 속에 넣거나 비닐랩으로 싸두고 김을 8×6인치로 잘라 준비한다. 김발 위에 김을 펴고 손에 물을 묻혀 밥을 반 컵 정도 얇게 펴준다. 붉은 깨를 조금 뿌리고 밥이 밑으로 가도록 뒤집은 후 그 위에 아보카도와 오이, 게살을 올리고 돌돌 만다. 랩으로 싸두었다가 먹기 직전에 랩을 벗기고 8등분한다. 접시에 담고 날치 알을 위에 얹어 장식하고 절인 생강과 와사비를 곁들인 간장과 함께 낸다.

{ Sushi Rice 초밥 }

Ingredients
- 2 cups Japanese short grain rice • 2 ¼ cups water
- 1 2x2 inch piece kombu • 1 tablespoon sake

Ingredients for Sushi Vinegar
- 5 tablespoons rice vinegar • 4 tablespoons sugar
- 1 tablespoon salt • 1 2x2 inch piece kombu • Juice from ¼ of a lemon

Heat a small sauce pan over low heat and add rice vinegar, sugar, and salt. Stir until the sugar dissolves and add kombu and lemon. Remove from heat and allow to cool to room temperature.

Put the rice in a large bowl and wash it with cold water. Repeat washing until the water becomes almost clear. Drain the rice in a colander and set aside for 30 minutes. Place the rice and kombu in a rice cooker and add water. Let the rice soak in the water for at least 30 minutes. Cook the rice in the rice cooker according to manufacturer's directions. When rice is cooked sprinkle the sake over the top and replace the lid, letting it steam for about 15 minutes.

Spread the hot steamed rice into a large non-metallic bowl. It is best to use a wooden bowl called sushi-oke. Sprinkle the vinegar mixture over the rice and fold the rice quickly. Using a fan to help cool and remove moisture from the sushi rice as you stir will improve the texture and give the sushi rice a shiny look. Use sushi rice right away.

재료 • 쌀 2컵 • 물 2 ¼컵 • 다시마(사방 4센티) 1조각 • 정종 1큰술 단촛물 재료 • 식초 5큰술 • 설탕 4큰술 • 소금 1큰술 • 다시마(사방 4센티) 1조각
• 레몬 ¼개, 즙을 낸다

작은 냄비에 식초, 설탕, 소금을 넣어 약한 불에 올려놓고, 설탕과 소금이 녹으면 다시마와 레몬을 넣고 불에서 내려 식힌다. 쌀에 찬물을 조금 부어 살살 문질러 씻은 다음 맑은 물이 나올 때까지 서너 번 더 씻어 체에 밭쳐 30분 정도 그대로 둔다. 쌀을 밥솥에 넣고 물을 부어 30분 정도 더 불린 다음 다시마 1조각과 물을 넣고 밥을 짓는다. 밥이 거의 다 되면 정종을 뿌리고 15분 정도 뜸을 들인다. 밥을 큰 그릇에 퍼서 단촛물을 붓고 뒤집어가며 재빨리 부채나 선풍기 바람으로 식혀 윤기가 나는 초밥을 완성한다.

Cold Shrimp and Noodle Salad with Wasabi Dressing 와사비 드레싱 소면샐러드

* Cook's Note: While I like to use somen noodles in this salad, you can use pretty much any kind of noodle. I have used soba noodles, udon noodles, and even spaghetti noodles for this salad and they have all worked out fine. This is also a great recipe to make when you want to use up any leftover fresh vegetables in your refrigerator.

Ingredients
• 2 bundles somen noodles • 10 large fresh shrimp
• 1 small cucumber, thinly sliced • 3 red radishes, thinly sliced
• 1 celery stalk, thinly sliced • ⅓ red bell pepper, chopped

Ingredients for Dressing
• 2 tablespoons soy sauce • 2 tablespoons sugar
• 2 tablespoons lemon juice or rice vinegar • 2 tablespoons sesame oil
• 1 teaspoon wasabi paste • 1 tablespoon green onion, chopped
• 1 teaspoon toasted sesame seeds

Mix all ingredients for wasabi dressing and set aside.

Cook somen noodles according to directions on the package and rinse with cold water, draining well. Wash shrimp, leaving shells on and carefully cut down the backbone of each shrimp and remove vein. Cook the shrimp in boiling water until they turn pink and are cooked through. Drain and set aside to cool. Peel and cut each shrimp in half, lengthwise. Arrange all of the prepared ingredients on a large serving plate and place noodles in the middle.

Add the dressing just before eating and mix together tableside.

Serves two.

재료(2인분) • 소면 2인분 • 생새우 큰 것 10개 • 작은 오이 1개, 얇게 썬다 • 래디시 3개, 얇게 썬다 • 셀러리 1줄기, 얇게 썬다 • 홍피망 ⅓개, 잘게 썬다 와사비 드레싱 재료 • 간장 2큰술 • 설탕 2큰술 • 레몬즙(또는 식초) 2큰술 • 참기름 2큰술 • 와사비 1작은술 • 다진 파 1큰술 • 볶은 깨 1작은술 드레싱 재료를 잘 섞어둔다.

소면은 포장지에 적힌 방법대로 삶아서 찬물에 헹궈 물기를 빼둔다. 새우는 내장을 제거하고 끓는 물에 삶아내 식혀서 껍질을 벗기고 길이로 반 갈라둔다. 접시 가운데에 국수를 놓고 준비한 재료를 둘러 담은 후 먹기 직전에 소스를 뿌려 무친다.

Cold Udon Noodle Salad 냉우동 샐러드

Udon salads are very popular in South Korea right now. It is not surprising that the hotter the weather, the more I crave this salad. The combination of the cool, chewy, udon noodles and the crisp, fresh vegetables make a satisfying yet refreshing meal. Just a cautionary note, be careful not to overcook the noodles, and rinse well to keep them from becoming gummy.

Ingredients

• 2 packages Japanese style udon noodles
• 2 cups mesclun greens • 10 fresh medium sized shrimp
• 2 pickling cucumbers or baby English cucumbers, cut into thin round slices
• 2 each mini red and yellow peppers, cut into thin round slices
• 3 red radishes, cut into thin round slices

Ingredients for Vinegar Soy Dressing

• 2 tablespoons soy sauce • 2 tablespoons sugar
• 2 tablespoons rice vinegar • 1 tablespoon oyster sauce
• 2 teaspoons wasabi • 4 tablespoons olive oil
• 1 tablespoon lemon juice • 1 tablespoon sesame oil
• 1 teaspoon garlic, minced

Mix all ingredients for vinegar soy dressing and set aside.

Wash the shrimp in cold water, leaving the shells on and carefully cut each shrimp down the backbone to remove the vein. Cook shrimp in boiling water until they turn pink and are cooked through. Be careful not to overcook the shrimp as they can become rubbery. Drain the shrimp and set aside to cool. Peel and cut each shrimp in half, lengthwise.

Bring 4 cups of water to a boil over medium-high heat and cook the udon noodles for 30 seconds. Rinse with cold water, draining well.

Pour ½ of the dressing onto the noodles and mix well. Arrange spring mix, shrimp, cucumbers, peppers, radishes and noodles on a large serving platter and pour more dressing over them to taste. Place noodles on top of the vegetables and shrimp and combine just before serving.

재료 • 일본식 우동 국수 2인분 • 스프링믹스 2컵 • 새우 중간 크기 10마리 • 작은 오이 2개, 둥글고 얇게 썬다 • 홍파프리카 2개, 둥글고 얇게 썬다 • 노랑 파프리카 2개, 둥글고 얇게 썬다 • 래디시 3개, 둥글고 얇게 썬다 비빔장 재료 • 간장 2큰술 • 설탕 2큰술 • 식초 2큰술 • 굴소스 1큰술 • 와사비 2작은술 • 올리브유 4큰술 • 레몬즙 1큰술 • 참기름 1큰술 • 다진 마늘 1작은술 비빔장 재료를 잘 섞어둔다.

새우는 찬물에 씻어 껍질째 등을 갈라 내장을 제거하고 끓는 물에 핑크색으로 변할 때까지 삶아 건져 식힌 다음 껍질을 벗겨 반으로 가른다. 냄비에 물 4컵을 넣고 끓으면 우동 국수를 넣어 30초 정도 삶아 건져 찬물에 헹궈 물기를 뺀다. 삶아낸 우동 국수에 비빔장의 반을 넣고 잘 섞어둔다. 접시에 스프링믹스를 깔고 우동 국수와 준비해둔 새우, 오이, 파프리카 등을 얹은 후 먹기 직전에 나머지 비빔장을 위에 끼얹어낸다.

One-Pot Seafood and Vegetable Rice (Yeongyang Sotbap)

영양솥밥

Yeongyang Sotbap is the ultimate seasonal recipe. It originated as a harvest food, and was typically made in the fall in Korea. This dish was meant to be made when all of the ingredients were being harvested and could be used in one dish. With various ingredients such as seafood, nuts, and vegetables, Yeongyang Sotbap is truly a one-pot meal. *Cook's Note: The sweet potato is not just a delicious surprise underneath all of the other ingredients; it also helps keep the rice from sticking to the bottom of the pot.

Ingredients

- 2 cups short grain rice, soaked in water for 3 hours
- 2 cups chicken stock • ½ pound oysters
- 10 shrimp • 10 chestnuts, cooked and peeled
- 2 dried Asian dates, slivered and any seeds removed
  (can be found in any Asian grocery store)
- 2 dried shitake mushrooms, soaked in warm water
  to reconstitute for 30 minutes, stems discarded and cut into thin strips.
- ½ cup peas • ¼ sweet potato, julienned
- 1 tablespoon sesame oil • 10 ginkgo nuts, shelled and blanched (optional)

Ingredients for Soy Dressing

- 2 tablespoons soy sauce • 1 tablespoon sugar
- 1 tablespoon rice vinegar • 1 tablespoon green onion, chopped
- 1 teaspoon garlic, minced • 1 teaspoon toasted sesame seeds
- 1 teaspoon hot pepper powder

Mix together all ingredients for Soy Dressing and set aside.

Wash shrimp and oysters in salted water and drain well. Oil the bottom of a large, thick bottomed pot. Add sweet potato and spread in an even layer over the bottom of the pot. Add rice, cooked seafood, and the additional ingredients, and gently flatten until spread over the sweet potato. Add sesame oil and chicken stock. Cover and bring to a boil over high heat. Let boil for about 5 minutes. Turn the heat down to medium and cook for another 5 minutes. Turn the heat down an additional time to the lowest setting and continue to cook for about 10 more minutes. Turn off the heat and let the pot sit, covered, for 5 more minutes. Remove the lid from the pot, fluff and mix the rice. Add the soy dressing to taste and mix together to eat. Makes 3 servings.

재료(3인분) • 불린 쌀 2컵, 물에 3시간 정도 불린 뒤 물기를 빼둔다 • 닭육수 2컵 • 굴 ½파운드 • 새우 10마리 • 밤 10알, 껍질을 벗겨 물에 담가둔다 • 대추 2알, 씨를 제거하고 썰어둔다 • 마른 표고버섯 2개, 미지근한 물에 30분간 불려 기둥을 떼고 채 썬다 • 고구마 ¼개, 채 썰어둔다 • 완두콩 ½ 컵 • 참기름 1큰술 • (선택) 은행 10알, 볶아서 껍질을 벗겨둔다 양념장 재료 • 간장 2큰술 • 설탕 1큰술 • 식초 1큰술 • 다진 파 1큰술 • 다진 마늘 1작은술 • 볶은 깨 1작은술 • 고춧가루 1작은술 양념장 재료를 잘 섞어둔다.

새우 살과 생굴은 연한 소금물에 흔들어 씻고 물기를 제거한다. 밑이 두꺼운 냄비에 기름을 바르고 채 썬 고구마를 깐 후 그 위에 불린 쌀과 준비해둔 재료들을 얹은 후 참기름과 닭육수를 부어 냄비뚜껑을 덮고 센 불로 5분 정도 끓인다. 중간 불로 줄이고 5분간 더 끓인 다음 밥물이 없어지면 제일 약한 불로 줄이고 10분간 뜸을 들인 후 불을 끄고 5분간 두었다 퍼서 양념장과 같이 낸다.

Sashimi Bibimbap (Hwe Dup Bap) 회덮밥

Sashimi Bibimbop is my husband's absolute favorite dish. He could happily eat it at least once a week, and my mom loves to make it for him every single time we go to visit. Luckily for him, it's also my dad's favorite dish, so there are no complaints at home about the frequency. Sashimi Bibimbop, or Hwe Dup Bap, is similar to the Japanese dish, Chirashi, which is sushi rice topped with sashimi. This version is similar, but seasoned more like a traditional bibimbap.

Ingredients

• 8 ounces sashimi-quality salmon, tuna or any other sashimi
• 3 tablespoons flying fish roe • I small cucumber, julienned
• I leaf red cabbage, julienned • I small carrot, peeled and julienned
• I inch thick slice daikon radish, peeled and sliced as thinly as possible.
  Soak in cold water for 10 minutes, drain and pat dry.
• 3 cups short grain rice, freshly cooked
• 2 tablespoons basic sauce (vinegar 5: sugar 4: salt I)
• 2 tablespoons sesame oil • Radish sprouts for garnish
• Crown daisy leaves for garnish (optional) • toasted sesame seeds

Ingredients for Bibim Sauce

• 4 tablespoons Korean hot pepper paste (gochujang) • 3 tablespoons sugar
• 3 tablespoons rice vinegar • I tablespoon lemon juice
• ½ teaspoon garlic, minced • I tablespoon toasted sesame seed

Place ingredients for Bibim Sauce in a small bowl and mix thoroughly. Set aside. Season cooked warm rice with basic sauce and sesame oil. Place one cup of seasoned rice into each serving bowl, preparing one bowl for each person. Take some of each vegetable and place on top of the rice. Arrange sashimi and fish roe on top of the vegetables and drizzle sesame oil over the contents of the bowl. Sprinkle toasted sesame seeds over each serving. Serve Bibim Sauce in a separate bowl and allow each person to add as much as they would like.

재료 • 각종 회 8온스, 잘게 한입 크기로 썰어둔다 • 날치 알 3큰술 • 작은 오이 1개, 채 썬다 • 채 썬 적양배추 1컵 • 당근 1개, 채 썬다 • 무 1인치 1토막, 가늘게 채 썰어 찬물에 10분간 담갔다가 물기를 뺀다 • 밥 3공기, 새로 지은 밥으로 준비한다 • 베이식 소스(식초5 : 설탕4 : 소금1) 2큰술 • 참기름 2큰술 • 무순 한줌 • (선택) 쑥갓 한줌, 잎 부분을 떼어 씻은 후 물기를 빼둔다 • 볶은 깨 약간   초고추장 • 고추장 4큰술 • 설탕 3큰술 • 식초 3큰술 • 레몬 즙 1큰술 • 다진 마늘 ½작은술 • 볶은 깨 1큰술   재료들을 잘 섞어둔다.

밥을 고슬고슬하게 지어 베이식 소스와 참기름을 넣어 잘 섞어서 식혀둔다. 밥을 그릇 3개에 나누어 담고, 그 위에 채소를 돌려 담은 후 준비해둔 회와 날치 알을 가운데 올리고 초고추장을 원하는 만큼 넣어 비벼 먹는다.

Sushi Hand Rolls 스시 핸드롤

Our family likes to call these "whatever I feel like" rolls. The format of this recipe allows people to pick and choose what fillings they would like for their individual hand rolls. In a family of picky eaters, this type of meal definitely helps keep the peace at dinnertime.

Ingredients

• 1 avocado, peeled, pitted and sliced into ¼-½ inch strips
• ½ English (hothouse) cucumber,
  peeled and cut into 3 inch strips
• 5 crab sticks
• 2 eggs, beaten with a generous pinch of salt,
  cooked into a sheet, and sliced into thin strips
• 3 sheets toasted nori, cut into quarters.
• 1 cup prepared sushi rice, cooked and
  mixed with 1 tablespoon Basic sauce (vinegar 5 : sugar 4: salt 1)
• 3 tablespoons flying fish roe(optional)
• Pickled ginger, for serving • Wasabi paste, for serving
• Soy sauce, for serving

Take a small amount of the sushi rice and using your hands, take the rice and form a rectangular shape. Hold a quarter sheet of nori shiny side down in the palm of one hand and place the shaped sushi rice on top. Place your filling diagonally across the rice, pointing towards the corner farthest away from you. Roll the nori around the rice and filling creating a cone. Serve with pickled ginger, wasabi and soy sauce.

　　Optional: You can also include scallions, carrots, smoked salmon, shrimp, cooked meats or whatever else you like, to customize your hand roll to your personal taste.

재료 • 아보카도 1개, 0.25~0.5인치 두께로 길게 썬다 • 오이 ½개, 껍질을 살짝 벗기고 3인치 (8cm) 길이로 썬다 • 게맛살 5개, 가늘게 썬다 • 달걀 2개, 풀어서 소금을 약간 넣고 지단을 부쳐 다른 재료와 같은 길이로 썬다 • 스시용 김 3장, 4등분한다 • 뜨거운 밥 1컵 + 베이식 소스 1큰술 (식초5 : 설탕4 : 소금1), 잘 섞어둔다 • (선택) 날치 알 3 큰술 • 생강 절임 · 와사비 · 간장

단촛물로 양념해둔 밥을 손에 쥐고 긴 타원형의 스시 모양을 만든다. 손바닥에 김을 올리고 그 위에 밥과 원하는 재료들을 얹어 콘 모양으로 말아 간장, 생강 절임, 와사비를 곁들여내거나 큰 접시에 준비해둔 재료들을 예쁘게 담아내고 각자 원하는 재료를 넣어 싸먹어도 좋다.
tip 파채, 당근채, 훈제 연어, 새우, 익힌 고기 등 원하는 재료들을 넣어 만들어도 좋다.

Vietnamese "Pho"
Rice Noodle Soup with Beef 월남 쌀국수

Last year my parents visited my brother Mike in California and tried Pho for the first time. They absolutely loved it and could not get enough. When they got back to Michigan, there were no good Pho restaurants to be found, so my mom decided to try to recreate it at home. She tried a dozen different recipes before landing on this one. She included it here for all you Pho lovers without any nearby restaurants to satisfy your craving. *Cook's Note: Do not neglect to char the onions and ginger, as it makes them sweeter and adds so much to the dish.

Ingredients

- 1 pound dried Vietnamese rice noodles, soaked in warm water for 20 minutes, then cooked and drained
- Beef brisket leftover from making the broth
- 12 large shrimp, cooked, peeled and deveined
- 1 cup mung bean sprouts • 1 cup cilantro • 1 cup thai basil
- 1 cup mint • 1 lime, cut into wedges • 2~3 jalapeño peppers, sliced
- ½ onion, thinly sliced and soaked in 2 tablespoons basic sauce
  (Basic sauce is made of 5 parts vinegar to 4 parts sugar to 1 part salt.)

Ingredients for Broth

- 1 ½ pounds beef brisket, flank steak, or shank • 16 cups water
- 1 onion, peeled, halved and charred
- 1 inch-sized piece of ginger, thinly sliced and lightly charred
- 1 cinnamon stick • 1 whole star anise • 1 tablespoon fish sauce
- 2 teaspoons sugar • 1 tablespoon salt

Soak the meat for the stock in cold water for 30 minutes and drain. In a large pot, bring 16 cups of water to a boil over medium high heat. Add the beef and bring back to a boil for 10 minutes. Skim the surface often to remove any foam and fat. Add the charred ginger and onions, fish sauce, salt and sugar. Simmer until the beef brisket is tender, about 1 hour.

Remove the beef from broth and set aside. Add star anise and cinnamon stick to the broth. Let infuse until the broth is fragrant, about 20 minutes, then strain the liquid through cheesecloth or a very fine mesh strainer. Pour broth back into the pot and continue to simmer, skimming as necessary, until you're ready to assemble the dish. Slice the boiled beef into thin slices. Place the cooked noodles and sliced beef into serving bowls. Ladle boiling broth into each bowl. Garnish with shrimp, onions, bean sprouts, chili peppers, cilantro, mint and basil. Serve immediately with lime wedges. Serves Four.

재료 • 마른 쌀국수 450g(1파운드), 미지근한 물에 20분 정도 담갔다가 끓는 물에 30초 정도 삶아 찬물에 헹구어 건져둔다 • 삶은 쇠고기, 얇게 썬다 • 새우 12마리, 내장을 제거하고 익혀서 껍질을 벗겨둔다 • 숙주 1컵, 다듬어 씻어둔다 • 고수 1컵, 깨끗이 씻어 물에 담가둔다 • 라임 1개, 6등분한다 • 청양고추 2~3개, 송송 썬다 • 양파 ½개 + 베이식 소스(식초5 : 설탕4 : 소금1) 2큰술, 얇게 썰어 베이식 소스를 부어둔다 • (선택) 바질, 민트 잎 국물 재료(4인분) • 쇠고기(양지머리) 또는 치맛살, 사태 700g • 물 16컵 • 양파 1개, 반 갈라 불에 구워둔다 • 생강 1토막, 얇게 썰어 불에 구워둔다 • 통계 피 1개 • 팔각 1개 • 액젓 1큰술 • 설탕 2작은술 • 소금 1큰술

쇠고기는 찬물에 30분 정도 담가 핏물을 빼둔다. 큰 냄비에 물 16컵을 넣고 중불에 올려 끓기 시작하면 쇠고기를 넣는다. 위에 뜨는 불순물이나 기름을 건져내며 10분간 끓인 다음 구운 양파, 생강, 액젓, 소금, 설탕을 넣고 고기가 푹 익을 때까지 약 1시간 정도 끓인다. 익은 고기는 건져내고 팔각과 통계피를 넣어 20분 정도 더 끓인 후 깨끗하게 체에 걸러 냄비에 넣고 약한 불에 올린다. 삶아놓은 국수를 나누어 그릇에 담고 뜨거운 국물을 부은 후 새우, 양파 절임, 숙주, 고추, 고수, 민트 잎, 바질 등 원하는 재료를 얹고 라임과 같이 낸다.
tip 양파와 생강을 불에 구우면 부드럽고 단맛이 나서 국물의 맛을 좋게 한다. 오븐팬에 놓아 브로일로 구워도 편리하다.

Noodles with Black Bean Sauce

(Jajangmyun) 자장면

One of the first tasks I take on when I move to a new area is to find the best local jajangmyun. There is just nothing like that dark, thick, black bean sauce over chewy noodles and the fresh, crisp, sweetness from the shredded cucumber. It is the ultimate comfort food and an extremely popular Korean Chinese fusion dish.

Ingredients

• 14 ounces fresh jajangmyun noodles or other pasta noodles
• ½ pound lean pork, cut into ½ inch cubes • I large onion, cut into ½ inch cubes
• I cup cabbage, cut into ½ inch cubes • I zucchini, cut into ½ inch cubes
• 6 tablespoons black bean paste • I ½ tablespoons sugar
• I tablespoon cornstarch + I tablespoon water, mixed well • I cup chicken stock or water
• 5 tablespoons canola oil or vegetable oil • I small cucumber, julienned

Heat canola oil in a large wok over high heat. Add the pork and stir fry until fully cooked. Add the vegetables and black bean paste. Cook until soft, about 2 minutes. Add chicken stock or water and sugar. Bring to a boil over high heat. Once the sauce comes to a boil, add cornstarch and water and quickly mix in. Lower the heat and simmer until the sauce thickens.

Boil water in a large pot and cook noodles until tender. Rinse with cold water several times, draining well. Portion the noodles into 3 large bowls and pour the black bean sauce over the noodles. Garnish with cucumber strips on top of the sauce and noodles and serve. Makes 2-3 servings.

재료 (2~3인분) • 생국수 2인분 • 돼지고기 230g(½파운드), 잘게 썬다 • 큰 양파 1개, 잘게 썬다 • 잘게 썬 양배추 1컵 • 호박 1개, 잘게 썬다 • 자장 소스 6큰술 • 설탕 1½큰술 • 전분 1큰술 + 물 1큰술 • 닭육수(또는 물) 1컵 • 카놀라유(또는 식용유) 5큰술 • 작은 오이 1개, 채 썬다

센 불에서 팬을 뜨겁게 달궈 기름을 넣고 돼지고기를 넣어 다 익을 때까지 볶다가 자장 소스와 준비해둔 채소들을 넣어 볶는다. 채소가 숨이 죽으면 육수와 설탕을 넣고 저으며 끓인다. 끓기 시작하면 녹말물을 넣어 재빨리 섞어 소스를 완성한다. 끓는 물에 국수를 넣고 삶아 찬물에 여러 번 헹궈 물기를 빼둔다. 준비된 국수를 그릇에 담고 뜨거운 소스를 부은 후 오이채를 얹어낸다.

Yangjangpi 양장피

Yangjangpi is served in most Korean Chinese restaurants in Korea. The noodles are made from green bean starch and have a chewy, distinct texture. It is often served on special occasions as a "fancier" alternative to the more commonly served japchae. The sheer number of ingredients and steps may be intimidating, but the interesting mix of cooked, raw, chewy, cold, and hot ingredients make a dish that is worth the effort.

Ingredients

- ⅓ pound pork loin, sliced into long, thin pieces
- ½ large onion, cut into very thin strips
- ½ zucchini, cut into very thin strips (use the harder, green, outer layer only)
- 2 dried shitake mushrooms, soaked in warm water
  to reconstitute for 30 minutes, stems discarded and cut into thin strips.
- ½ cup chives, cut into 2 inch pieces
- ½ of a yellow bell pepper, cut into very thin strips
- 10 large cooked shrimp, peeled and cut in half, lengthwise
- 1 squid (body only, no legs), cut open and cleaned
- 2 eggs, beaten • 1 carrot, cut into thin strips 2 inches long
- 1 cucumber, seeded and cut into thin strips 2 inches long
- 3 radishes, cut into strips • 2 green bean starch sheets
- 1 tablespoon sesame oil • 1 tablespoon soy sauce • canola oil

Ingredients for Pork Marinade

- 1 tablespoon oyster sauce • 1 tablespoon mirin • ½ teaspoon cornstarch
- ¼ teaspoon black pepper • 3 tablespoons canola oil

Ingredients for Stir-Fry Sauce

- 1 teaspoon chopped ginger • 2 cloves of garlic, thinly sliced
- 1 tablespoon soy sauce • 1 tablespoon mirin
- 1 teaspoon sugar • 1 tablespoon sesame oil
- ¼ teaspoon salt • ¼ teaspoon black pepper

Ingredients for Mustard Sauce

- ⅓ cup chicken broth + ½ teaspoon cornstarch, mixed well
- 1 tablespoon Asian hot mustard
- 3 tablespoons basic sauce (vinegar 5: sugar 4: salt 1)
- 1 tablespoon sesame oil • ⅛ teaspoon black pepper

Make mustard sauce by bringing chicken broth and cornstarch to a boil in a small saucepan, adding Asian hot mustard and mixing well. Let mustard ferment in the broth for 10 minutes. Add basic sauce, sesame oil, black pepper and mix thoroughly. Set aside.

In a medium sized bowl, add ingredients for pork marinade and mix thoroughly. Add pork and combine, being sure that each piece is coated. Set aside.

Soak green bean starch sheets in warm water for 10 minutes. Cook in boiling water until soft. Drain and rinse in cold water. Tear each sheet into small pieces and marinate with 1 tablespoon of sesame oil and 1 tablespoon of soy sauce.

Prepare the squid by using the tip of a knife to score the side of the squid that curls inward in a crisscross pattern. Bring a large pot of water to a boil. Add squid and cook until it just starts to curl, about 3 minutes. Drain and slice into ¼ inch round pieces

Grease a frying pan with oil and heat over medium low heat. Add beaten eggs and cook slowly, tilting pan to create a thin sheet of cooked egg. Remove from pan and slice thinly.

Heat a wok over high heat and add 2 tablespoons of canola oil. Add minced garlic and ginger and cook for about 10 seconds. Add marinated pork and stir-fry until just cooked. Add onion, zucchini, shitake mushrooms, chives and yellow bell peppers. Stir-fry until vegetables are cooked and add soy sauce, mirin, sugar and sesame oil. Add salt and pepper to taste.

Place green bean starch pieces in the middle of a serving platter and pour stir-fried pork and vegetables over them. Arrange shrimp, cooked squid, egg strips, carrot, cucumber and radish decoratively around the edge of the plate. Add the mustard sauce right before serving.

볶음 재료 • 돼지고기 ⅓파운드, 굴소스 1큰술, 맛술 1큰술, 전분 ½작은술, 후추¼작은술, 카놀라유 3큰술을 넣어 밑간해둔다 • 양파 ½개, 채 썬다 • 호박 ½개, 돌려깎기해서 파란 부분만 채 썬다 • 표고버섯 2장, 미지근한 물에 30분 정도 불려서 채 썬다 • 부추 ½컵, 5센티 길이로 썬다 • 노랑 피망 ½개, 채 썬다 볶음 양념 재료 • 다진 생강 1작은술 • 마늘 2개, 얇게 썬다 • 간장 1큰술 • 맛술 1큰술 • 설탕 1작은술 • 참기름 1큰술 • 후추 ¼작은술 • 소금 ¼작은술 • 카놀라유 돌림 재료 • 새우 10마리, 내장을 제거하고 데쳐서 껍질을 벗겨 반을 갈라둔다 • 오징어(몸통) 1마리, 칼집을 넣어 데쳐서 ¼인치 두께로 둥글게 썬다 • 달걀 2개, 풀어서 지단으로 부쳐 5센티 길이로 채 썬다 • 당근 1개, 껍질을 벗기고 5센티 길이로 채 썬다 • 오이 1개, 껍질 부분만 돌려깎기해서 5센티 길이로 채 썬다 • 래디시 3개, 채 썬다 • 양장피 2장, 따뜻한 물에 담갔다가 끓는 물에 5분간 삶아 찬물에 헹궈 물기를 뺀다. 먹기 좋은 크기로 잘라 참기름과 간장으로 밑간해둔다 • 참기름 1큰술 • 간장 1큰술

달군 팬에 기름을 두르고 썰어둔 생강과 마늘을 넣어 향이 우러나면 밑간해둔 고기를 넣어 볶아 어느 정도 익혀준다. 거기에 준비해둔 볶음 재료들을 넣어 볶아주고 볶음 양념으로 양념해둔다. 큰 접시에 준비해둔 돌림 재료를 예쁘게 돌려 담고, 밑간해둔 양장피를 가운데에 깔고 그 위에 볶아둔 재료들을 얹어 겨자 소스와 함께 낸다. 소스는 먹기 바로 전에 끼얹어야 더 맛있다.

겨자 소스 재료 • 닭육수 ⅓컵 + 전분 ½작은술 • 겨자 1큰술 • 베이식 소스 3큰술(식초5 : 설탕4 : 소금1) • 참기름 1큰술 • 후추 ⅛작은술

닭육수에 전분을 섞어 살짝 끓여 걸쭉해지면 뜨거울 때 겨자를 개서 숙성시킨 다음 베이식 소스, 참기름, 후추를 섞어 소스를 만들어둔다.

Shrimp and Chicken Fried Rice 새우 닭고기 볶음밥

The key to this tasty fried rice is the chicken stock. It seasons the rice, which is the main body of the dish, and provides a lot of flavor in addition to all of the other ingredients. *Cook's Note: Do not use sticky rice, as it will clump. Using long grain rice will ensure fluffy fried rice.

Ingredients

- 2 cups long grain rice
- 10 medium shrimp, shelled and cut into ½ inch cubes
- ⅓ pound boneless chicken breast, cut into ½ inch cubes
- 2 eggs, lightly beaten
- 3 shitake mushrooms, soaked in warm water to reconstitute for 30 minutes, stems discarded, and cut into small cubes.
- ½ cup cooked peas • ½ cup chicken stock
- 1 tablespoon of rice wine • 1 teaspoon salt
- ¼ teaspoon black pepper • 4 tablespoons canola oil
- 1 tablespoon sesame oil

Put rice in a large bowl and wash it with cold water. Rinse the rice with water until the water becomes almost clear. Drain the rice in a colander and set aside for 10 minutes. Put rice in a rice cooker and add 2 ¼ cups water. Close the lid of rice cooker and turn it on.

Heat 1 tablespoon of canola oil in a large frying pan over medium high heat. Sauté shrimp until it turns pink. Sprinkle with a little salt to taste. Remove from pan and set aside. Add another tablespoon of canola oil to the pan and quickly sauté chicken over high heat until fully cooked. Remove and set aside.

Heat 1 tablespoon of canola oil in a clean frying pan and cook beaten eggs quickly, stirring constantly to scramble.

Heat 2 tablespoons canola oil and 1 tablespoon sesame oil in large frying pan over medium heat. Add mushroom, shrimp, chicken, and rice. Sprinkle with rice wine, salt and pepper. Quickly sauté for a few minutes, then add boiled peas, scrambled eggs and chicken stock, mixing thoroughly and quickly over high heat. Serve warm. Makes four servings.

재료(4인분) • 쌀 2컵 • 새우 10마리, 껍질과 내장을 제거하고 0.5인치 크기로 썬다 • 닭가슴살 ⅓파운드, 0.5인치 크기로 썬다 • 달걀 2개, 잘 풀어둔다 • 마른 표고버섯 3장, 미지근한 물에 30분 정도 불려서 0.5인치 크기로 썬다 • 익힌 완두콩 ½컵 • 닭육수 ½컵 • 청주 1큰술 • 소금 1작은술 • 후추 ¼작은술 • 카놀라유 4큰술 • 참기름 1큰술

쌀은 찬물에 잘 씻어 물기를 뺀 후 10분 정도 그대로 둔다. 밥솥에 불린 쌀과 물 2 ¼컵을 넣고 고슬고슬하게 밥을 짓는다. 팬을 달구어 기름을 1큰술 두르고 새우를 넣어 볶아내어 소금으로 간을 하고, 다시 팬을 달구어 기름을 1큰술 넣고 재빨리 닭고기를 넣어 볶는다. 깨끗한 팬에 기름을 두르고 풀어둔 달걀을 넣어 저어가며 익혀 접시에 담는다. 커다란 팬을 달구어 카놀라유 2큰술과 참기름 1큰술을 넣고 표고버섯, 새우, 닭고기, 밥을 넣고 그 위에 청주, 소금, 후추를 넣고 볶은 후 완두콩, 달걀, 닭육수를 넣어 센 불로 볶아내어 뜨겁게 낸다.

tip 찰기가 적은 안남미로 만들어야 더 맛있다.

Noodles Soup with Oysters (Oyster Jjambong) 굴 짬뽕

When my mom was a child, jjambong was usually a white soup, not the red, spicy soup served in most restaurants today. The spiciness of the soup came from sliced green chilies, rather than hot red pepper, creating a lighter broth. While mom was in Korea, my uncle took her to a Chinese restaurant that served a white jjambong made with oysters. This jjambong reminded her of the jjambong of her childhood and inspired her to recreate it for this book.

Ingredients

• 2 package udon noodles • 1 pound oysters, washed with salt water and drained
• 20 large shrimp, peeled and deveined • 10 chives, cut into 2 inch pieces
• 1 onion, julienned • 1 zucchini, julienned • 2 green chilies, sliced into rounds
• 2 cups bean sprouts, washed and drained • 1 clove garlic, thinly sliced
• 1 green onion, chopped • 2 tablespoons oyster sauce
• 8 cups chicken stock or beef bone stock, heated • 2 tablespoons canola oil

Cook noodles in a large pot of boiling salted water until tender, stirring occasionally to keep the noodles from sticking. Drain and rinse in cold water. Portion the noodles into two serving bowls and add one cup of fresh bean sprouts to each bowl. Heat 1 tablespoon of canola oil in a frying pan over high heat and add garlic and green onion. Cook for 10 seconds. Add vegetables and stir-fry for 2 minutes. Add oyster sauce and mix to combine. Then add oysters, shrimp and hot chicken stock and bring to a rolling boil for about 2 more minutes. When seafood is fully cooked, pour the hot soup over cooked noodles and bean sprouts. Makes two servings.

재료(2인분) • 우동 면 2인분 • 굴 1파운드, 소금물에 살살 흔들어 씻어 물기를 빼둔다 • 새우 20마리, 껍질과 내장을 제거하고 깨끗이 손질해둔다 • 부추 10줄기, 5센티 길이로 썬다 • 양파 1개, 채 썬다 • 호박 1개, 채 썬다 • 청고추 2개, 둥글게 썬다 • 숙주 2컵, 씻어 물기를 뺀다 • 마늘 1개, 편으로 채 썬다 • 파 1뿌리, 채 썬다 • 굴소스 2큰술 • 닭뼈육수(또는 사골육수) 8컵 • 카놀라유 2큰술

닭뼈를 푹 끓여 육수를 만들어 간을 맞춘 후 약한 불로 계속 끓이고, 우동 면을 삶아 찬물에 헹궈 물기를 빼고 그릇에 담는다. 깨끗이 씻어 물기를 뺀 숙주를 넉넉히 면 위에 얹어 준비해둔다. 팬에 기름을 두르고 달군 다음 마늘과 파를 넣어 향을 내고 썰어놓은 부추, 호박, 양파, 청고추를 넣어 센 불에서 빨리 볶아내어 굴소스로 간을 한 후 굴과 새우를 넣고 뜨거운 육수를 부어 끓인다. 해물이 익으면 국수 위에 재빨리 부어서 낸다.

pork

Chinese Dumplings (Mul Mandu) 중국식 물만두

This is my favorite way to prepare dumplings. Most people prefer to fry dumplings, but I feel like the crispy fried skin can be greasy at times, and take away from the star of the show, the filling. When you boil the dumplings, the skin becomes a vehicle for the savory, juicy filling.

Ingredients
• 1 ½ cup ground pork • 1 cup chives, chopped
• 1 cup napa cabbage, chopped • ½ cup onion, chopped
• 1 teaspoon ginger juice • 2 tablespoons soy sauce
• 1 tablespoon rice wine or mirin • Salt and pepper
• 1 tablespoon water • 1 tablespoon sesame oil
• 1 package thin dumpling skins

Ingredients for Dipping Sauce
• 2 tablespoons soy sauce • 1 tablespoon sugar
• 2 tablespoons rice vinegar • 1 teaspoon green onion, chopped

Mix together all ingredients for dipping sauce and set aside.

Place ground pork or beef in a medium sized bowl and add ginger juice, soy sauce, rice wine, sesame oil, salt and pepper, stirring in only one direction to combine until the meat is sticky. Scald the chopped chives, Napa cabbage and onion in boiling water, drain, and squeeze tightly to drain of excess water. Add chives, cabbage and onion mixture to the meat, stirring in the same direction, and mix well.

Place about 1 tablespoon of the filling into the middle of a dumpling skin. Wet the edges of the skin with water or egg white. Fold the skin over the filling into a half moon shape and pinch the edges to seal. Continue with the remainder of the filling and dumpling skins.

To cook, bring a large pot of water to a boil. Add half the dumplings, giving them a gentle stir so they don't stick together. Bring the water back to a boil, and add ½ cup of cold water. Cover and repeat. When the dumplings come to a boil for a third time, they are ready. Drain and remove.

Makes about 30 dumplings.

재료(4인분) • 다진 돼지고기 1 ½컵 • 다진 중국부추 1컵 • 다진 배추 1컵 • 다진 양파 ½컵 • 생강즙 1작은술 • 간장 2큰술 • 청주 또는 맛술 1큰술 • 소금, 후추 약간 • 물 1큰술 • 참기름 1큰술 • 얇은 만두피 50장 소스 재료 • 간장 2큰술 • 설탕 1큰술 • 식초 2큰술 • 다진 파 1작은술 재료를 잘 섞어준다.

다진 돼지고기에 생강즙, 간장, 맛술, 참기름, 소금, 후추를 넣고 한쪽 방향으로 잘 섞어서 어느 정도 끈기가 생기면 물을 조금씩 넣으면서 다시 한 번 섞어준다. 다진 부추, 배추, 양파는 끓는 물에 살짝 데쳐 꼭 짜서 고기와 잘 섞어준다. 속이 만들어지면 준비해둔 얇은 만두피에 속을 한 스푼씩 넣어 만두를 빚는다. 만두를 팔팔 끓는 물에 넣고 삶아 끓어오르면 찬물을 반 컵 붓고, 다시 끓어 오르면 찬물을 조금 붓는 것을 서너 번 반복해준다. 익으면 건져내어 찬물에 헹궈 물기를 빼고 접시에 담아 소스와 함께 낸다.

Pan-Fried Tofu with Eggplant and Pork Sauce 두부구이와 가지 고기 소스

My mom often draws inspiration from childhood memories. By recreating dishes from her past, she is able to share those memories with us. This recipe is inspired by a dish my mom often ate while growing up in South Korea. The original dish was composed of cooked eggplant stuffed with a spicy meat sauce, similar in style to stuffed cucumber kimchi. This version is simpler to make but stays true to the flavors and ingredients of the original.

Ingredients

• I pound firm tofu, cut into pieces 2x3 inches long and ½ inch thick
• ¼ teaspoon salt • 2 tablespoons canola oil

Ingredients for Eggplant and Pork Sauce

• I eggplant, cut into ¼ inch cubes • ½ pound ground pork
• ½ medium size onion, chopped
• I ½ tablespoons gocuhjang (Korean hot pepper paste)
• I ½ tablespoons doenjang (Korean soy bean paste)
• I tablespoon sugar • I tablespoon rice wine
• I teaspoon garlic, minced • 2 tablespoons green onion, chopped
• I tablespoon toasted sesame seeds • 2 teaspoons sesame oil
• 2 tablespoons water

Place tofu on a large baking sheet lined with paper towels. Sprinkle salt evenly over the tofu pieces. Heat canola oil in a large frying pan over medium high heat. Fry tofu until golden brown, about three minutes on each side. Remove from pan and set aside.

Heat sesame oil in a large frying pan over medium heat and add chopped onion and ground pork. Add rice wine and sauté until pork is fully cooked and onion is softened. Add all of the rest of the sauce ingredients and mix together. Cook for a few more minutes to allow ingredients to meld. Transfer fried tofu to a plate, pour meat sauce over the tofu, garnish with chopped green onion and serve.

재료 • 두부 1파운드, 3×5센티에 1센티 두께로 썬다 • 소금 ¼작은술 • 카놀라유 2큰술 가지 고기 소스 재료 • 가지 1개, 작게 깍뚝썰기한다 • 다진 돼지고기 ½파운드 • 양파 ½개, 잘게 다진다 • 고추장 1 ½큰술 • 된장 1 ½큰술 • 설탕 1큰술 • 청주 1큰술 • 다진 마늘 1작은술 • 다진 파 2큰술 • 볶은 깨 1큰술 • 참기름 2작은술 • 물 2큰술

썰어놓은 두부에 소금을 뿌려둔다. 팬을 달구어 기름을 두르고 두부를 앞뒤로 노릇하게 3분씩 지져낸다. 중간 불로 달군 팬에 참기름을 두르고 다진 양파, 고기와 청주를 넣어 볶아준다. 고기와 양파가 익으면 나머지 재료들을 넣고 잘 섞어 다시 한 번 볶아준다. 큰 접시에 지진 두부를 놓고 그 위에 소스를 부은 다음 다진 파로 장식하여 낸다.

Pork Tonkatsu
with Balsamic Dressing 돈가스와 발사믹 드레싱

Growing up, my mom always dipped her tonkatsu in a mixture of vinegar and soy sauce. While I do enjoy the vinegary kick of that type of sauce, I tend to prefer the pre-made tonkatsu sauce you can buy at the grocery store. Pre-made tonkatsu sauce is sweeter, and I love the contrast of the sweet sauce and the crispy richness of the fried pork. This recipe combines the best of both worlds. The balsamic provides that sweetness I crave along with a tart kick that brightens up the whole dish.

Ingredients

- 4 slices of pork loin, about 4 ounces each, pounded thin
- ½ teaspoon sea salt
- ¼ teaspoon freshly ground black pepper
- 2 eggs, lightly beaten
- 1 ½ cup panko bread crumbs
- ½ cup flour for dredging
- 2 cups canola oil, for frying
- 2 cups cooked short grain rice mixed with 2 tablespoons of basic sauce
  while hot and fluffed to remove excess moisture (optional)
- 2 cups salad greens (optional)

Ingredients for Balsamic Dressing

- 1 cup balsamic vinegar • 1 tablespoon sugar (optional)

Pour balsamic vinegar into a small saucepan over high heat. Bring to a boil and lower the heat to medium low. Simmer until it is reduced by half, or until syrupy, whisking constantly to prevent burning. Allow to cool. If you like a very sweet reduction, sprinkle in a tablespoon of sugar and whisk until completely dissolved.

Season pork cutlets with salt and pepper. Put flour in a large bowl and dredge pork until all surfaces are lightly covered. Tap off the excess flour and dip each cutlet in the beaten eggs, coating thoroughly, and then dip into the panko. Be sure that both sides are covered well. Set aside or refrigerate for later.

Heat the canola oil in a heavy frying pan over high heat until hot. Add one pork cutlet, lower the heat slightly and cook until both sides are golden brown or until the pork is cooked through, about 2-3 minutes each side. Remove from the pan and drain on a paper towel. Repeat until all of the pork is cooked.

Arrange Tonkatsu, salad greens and rice on a serving plate and pour the balsamic dressing over them to taste.

재료 • 돼지고기 등심 4조각(4온스짜리), 두들겨 넓게 편다 • 바다소금 ½작은술 • 후추 ¼작은술 • 달걀 2개, 잘 풀어둔다 • 빵가루 1 ½컵 • 밀가루 ½컵 • 카놀라유 2컵(튀김용) 선택 재료 • 밥 2공기 + 베이식 소스 2큰술, 밥이 뜨거울 때 잘 섞어둔다 • 샐러드용 상추 2컵 발사믹 드레싱 재료 • 발사믹 식초 1컵 • (선택) 설탕 1큰술

작은 냄비에 발사믹 식초를 넣고 센 불에 올려 끓기 시작하면 불을 약하게 줄여 시럽이 될 때까지 타지 않도록 저으면서 졸인다. 달콤한 발사믹 드레싱을 원하면 설탕을 1큰술 넣어도 좋다. 준비해둔 돼지고기에 소금과 후추로 밑간을 하고 밀가루를 가볍게 묻힌다. 풀어놓은 달걀에 담갔다 건져 빵가루를 골고루 두둑하게 묻혀둔다. 미리 만들어 냉장보관해도 좋다. 두꺼운 튀김 냄비에 카놀라유를 넣고 센 불에 달궈 기름이 뜨거워지면 중간 불로 낮추고 준비해둔 돼지고기를 넣어 2~3분 정도 튀기고 뒤집어서 2~3분 정도 더 튀겨준다. 고기가 잘 익으면 종이타월 위에 건져내 기름을 뺀다. 접시에 돈가스를 담고 옆에 밥과 샐러드를 곁들여 발사믹 드레싱을 뿌려낸다.

Kimchi Pancakes 김치전

This recipe is one of my favorites out of this entire collection. I have great memories of sitting in my mom's kitchen, waiting eagerly as she scooped kimchi pancake batter from a blue mixing bowl and made perfect circles with it on a large griddle. After each one was done, she would flip them on to a plate lined with paper towels and hand me a fresh one, still hot from the griddle. I would eat it slowly, savoring the crispy edges, the meaty, savory pork bits, and the spicy, softened kimchi. While making them myself doesn't have quite the same effect, eating these fresh from the frying pan brings me straight back to that time in my mom's kitchen.

Ingredients
- 2 cups cabbage kimchi, chopped
- ⅓ pound ground pork
- 1 ½ cups flour • 1 ¼ cups water
- ½ cup green onions, chopped
- 1 egg, lightly beaten
- ½ cup soybean sprouts, trimmed and cut in half
- ½ cup canola oil for frying

Combine ground pork, kimchi, soybean sprouts, flour, chopped green onion, egg, and 1 cup of water in a bowl, mixing well. Set aside to rest for 10 minutes. Heat 2 tablespoons of canola oil in a non-stick skillet over medium high heat. Pour ½ cup of batter into the skillet and cook for about 3 minutes or until edges are crispy, flattening it as it cooks. Flip and cook until golden brown on both sides. Clean the pan with paper towel, add 1-2 tablespoons of oil and repeat with the rest of the batter, adding more oil in between each batch. Transfer pancakes to serving plate and serve warm. Makes four servings.

재료(4인분) • 잘게 썬 김치 2컵 • 다진 돼지고기 ⅓파운드 • 밀가루 1 ½컵 • 물 1 ¼컵 • 다진 파 ½컵 • 달걀 1개, 잘 풀어둔다 • 콩나물 ½컵, 끝을 다듬어서 길이로 2등분한다 • 카놀라유 ½컵 (부침용)

큰 그릇에 모든 재료를 넣고 잘 섞어 10분간 둔다. 중간 불로 달군 팬에 기름을 2큰 술 넣고 섞어둔 재료를 ½컵 정도 넣고 둥글고 얇게 펴서 3분 정도 지진다. 테두리 가 바삭하게 지져지면 뒤집어서 밑이 노릇해질 때까지 더 지져준다. 매번 종이타월 로 팬을 깨끗이 닦아내고 기름을 1~2큰술씩 더 넣어야 깨끗하게 지져진다. 뜨거울 때 접시에 담아낸다.

Stir-Fried Pork and Peppers with Steamed Buns 피망잡채와 꽃빵

I absolutely love steamed buns. Put any filling inside of a steamed bun, and even if it is made of something I do not like, I will eat the whole thing and enjoy it. The soft, white, fluffy buns are ideal for any type of filling, both sweet and savory. In fact, my favorite breakfast items are steamed buns filled with egg custard, which I always order at dim sum restaurants. For this particular dish, you can unroll the pre-made steamed buns and wrap them around the pork and peppers, or eat them separately. Personally, I like to unwrap the buns and tear them into small pieces, eating them bit by bit. I eat a piece of bun, take a bite of pork and peppers, use another piece of bun to soak up the delicious juices, and repeat.

Ingredients
- ½ pound pork loin, sliced into long, thin pieces
- I green bell pepper, cut into thin strips
- I red bell pepper, cut into thin strips
- ½ large onion, thinly sliced • I garlic clove, thinly sliced
- I package steamed buns • 2 tablespoons canola oil
- I cup cabbage, shredded, soaked in cold water and drained

Ingredients for Pork Marinade
- I tablespoon mirin • ⅛ teaspoon salt • ⅛ teaspoon black pepper

Ingredients for Sauce
- I tablespoon oyster sauce • I teaspoon soy sauce
- ½ teaspoon cornstarch + I teaspoon water, mixed well • I tablespoon sesame oil

Mix together ingredients for marinade, pour over the pork and set aside. Heat canola oil in a wok over medium-high heat. Add the sliced garlic and pork and stir-fry, stirring constantly, until the pork is just cooked through, about 2 to 3 minutes. Add the red and green bell pepper and onion. Continue to stir-fry until the onion is softened. Add the oyster sauce and soy sauce and cook for another minute or so. Stir cornstarch mixture into the pork and vegetables, and allow the sauce to thicken slightly. Remove from heat and add sesame oil, mixing well. Garnish with shredded cabbage and serve with steamed buns. Makes two servings.

재료(2인분) • 돼지고기 ½파운드(230g), 가늘게 채 썬다 • 청피망 1개, 씨를 빼고 가늘게 채 썬다 • 홍피망 1개, 씨를 빼고 가늘게 채 썬다 • 큰 양파 ½개, 가늘게 채 썬다 • 마늘 1개, 얇게 썬다 • 꽃빵 1봉지 • 카놀라유 2큰술 • 채 썬 양배추 1컵, 찬물에 담갔다가 물기를 뺀다 고기 밑간 재료 • 맛술 1큰술 • 소금 ⅛작은술 • 후추 ⅛작은술 소스 재료 • 굴소스 1큰술 • 간장 1작은술 • 전분 ½작은술 + 물 1작은술, 잘 섞는다 • 참기름 1큰술

돼지고기는 밑간 양념을 넣어 재워둔다. 달군 팬에 기름을 두르고 마늘을 넣어 향이 우러나면 돼지고기를 넣어 2~3분간 볶아준다. 어느 정도 익으면 채 썰어둔 채소를 넣어 한 번 더 볶아준다. 양파가 투명해지면 굴소스와 간장을 넣고 1분간 더 볶은 후 물에 녹인 전분을 넣어 약간 걸쭉해지면 마지막으로 참기름을 넣어 완성한다. 꽃빵을 찜기에 넣어 쪄낸 후 피망잡채, 양배추채와 함께 낸다.

Mapo Tofu 마파두부

Mapo Tofu is a spicy mix of tofu and ground pork that is often served over freshly cooked rice. The starchiness of the rice provides just the right counterpart to the spiciness of the sauce. Although the Mapo Tofu can be eaten alone or as a side dish, adding the rice creates a more complete meal. *Cook's Note: Be careful not to cut the pieces of tofu too small, as they will continue to break up as the dish cooks.

Ingredients
• I pound medium tofu, cubed • ⅓ pound ground pork
• 3 tablespoons green onion, chopped • 2 teaspoons minced garlic
• I teaspoon minced ginger • I red chili, seeded and chopped
• I green chili, seeded and chopped • ½ cup cooked green peas, drained
• 3 tablespoons canola oil • 2 tablespoons doubanjiang (chili bean paste)
• I cup chicken stock • I tablespoon rice wine
• I teaspoon soy sauce • ½ tablespoon sugar
• ⅛ teaspoon black pepper • I teaspoon oyster sauce
• I tablespoon cornstarch + 2 tablespoons water, mixed well
• I teaspoon sesame oil

Heat I tablespoon of canola oil in a large frying pan over medium heat. Add tofu and cook until lightly browned. Remove from pan and set aside. Add 2 tablespoons of oil to the pan and cook minced garlic, ginger, green onion, and red and green chili peppers and stir-fry over low heat for about 10 seconds. Increase the heat to high and add the ground pork, breaking it up as it browns, until the pork is just cooked through, about 2 to 3 minutes. Add the tofu, green peas, doubanjiang (chili bean paste), rice wine, and soy sauce and continue to cook for another 30 seconds.

Stir in the chicken stock and bring to a boil. Add the oyster sauce, sugar and black pepper to taste. Reduce heat to medium low and simmer for 2 minutes. Stir the cornstarch slurry into the simmering tofu to thicken the sauce slightly. Add sesame oil to taste and serve. Makes four servings.

재료(4인분) • 두부 한 모, 사방 1.5센티로 썰어 물기를 뺀다 • 다진 돼지고기 ⅓파운드(150g) • 다진 파 3큰술 • 다진 마늘 2작은술 • 다진 생강 1작은술 • 홍고추 1개, 씨를 빼고 다진다 • 매운 청고추 1개, 씨를 빼고 다진다 • 삶은 완두콩 ½컵, 물기를 뺀다 • 카놀라유 3큰술 • 두반장 2큰술 • 닭육수 1컵 • 청주 1큰술 • 간장 1작은술 • 설탕 ½큰술 • 후추 ⅛작은술 • 굴소스 1작은술 • 전분 1큰술 + 물 2큰술, 잘 풀어둔다 • 참기름 1작은술

달군 팬에 기름을 1큰술 두르고 썰어둔 두부를 살짝 지져낸다. 다른 팬을 달구어 나머지 기름을 두르고 다진 생강, 파, 마늘, 고추를 넣고 약한 불에서 볶아 매운 향이 나면 불을 세게 하고 다진 돼지고기를 넣어 덩어리가 지지 않게 저어가며 볶는다. 고기가 어느 정도 익으면 두부와 완두콩, 두반장, 청주, 간장을 넣어 간이 배도록 볶은 후 육수를 부어 한소끔(3분 정도) 끓여 굴소스, 설탕, 후추로 맛을 낸다. 풀어놓은 전분을 넣어 걸쭉해지면 참기름을 넣어 완성한다.

Pork and Kimchi Kabobs 돼지고기 김치산적

Pork and kimchi is such a great combination that I am always looking for new ways to cook them together. The savory richness of the pork is nicely balanced by the pickled, spicy kimchi. These kabobs are easy to make, delicious, and aesthetically pleasing. *Cook's Note: Use whole napa cabbage kimchi in order to ensure you can cut the proper sized pieces. Napa cabbage kimchi often comes chopped, but the pieces tend to be too small for these kabobs. Additionally, be sure to use the white part of the kimchi and not the leaves as they do not hold up well when grilled.

Ingredients

- $\frac{1}{2}$ pound pork loin, cut into $\frac{1}{4} \times \frac{1}{2} \times 3$ inch strips
- $\frac{1}{2}$ pound whole napa cabbage kimchi (white part only), cut into $\frac{1}{2} \times 3$ inch strips
- I teaspoon sugar • I teaspoon sesame oil
- 10 green onions, cut into 3 inch pieces
- $\frac{1}{4}$ cup flour • I egg • Canola oil for frying

Ingredients for Pork Marinade

- I teaspoon soy sauce • I teaspoon rice wine
- $\frac{1}{2}$ teaspoon garlic, minced • I teaspoon ginger juice
- $\frac{1}{2}$ teaspoon sugar • 2 teaspoons sesame oil

Additional Equipment

- 10 bamboo skewers

Put kimchi in a large bowl and sprinkle sugar and sesame oil over the top. Combine all ingredients for Pork Marinade in a small bowl. Pour marinade over pork and let it sit for 10 minutes. Place pork, kimchi, and green onions in alternating layers on the bamboo skewers. You can order the ingredients any way you wish.

Put flour in a separate bowl and dip each skewer until lightly covered on one side. Heat 2 teaspoons of oil in large skillet over medium heat. While the pan heats, lightly beat the egg with a pinch of salt. Dip each skewer into the beaten egg, and place directly into the hot pan. Cook until pork is cooked through and both sides are light brown. It should take about 2 or 3 minutes per side. Periodically refresh the pan with new oil and repeat the process for the rest of the skewers.

재료 • 돼지고기 등심 ½파운드(225g), 0.25 × 0.25 × 3인치로 썬다 • 포기김치 흰 부분 225g, 0.5 × 3인치로 썬다. • 설탕 1작은술 • 참기름 1작은술 • 실파 10개, 3인치 길이로 썬다 • 밀가루 ¼컵 • 달걀 1개, 잘 풀어둔다 • 카놀라유(부침용) • 꼬치 10개 고기 밑간 재료 • 간장 1작은술 • 청주 1작은술 • 다진 마늘 ½작은술 • 생강즙 1작은술 • 설탕 ½작은술 • 참기름 2작은술

김치를 설탕과 참기름으로 밑간해두고, 고기에 고기 양념장을 부어 10분간 재워둔다. 꼬치에 고기와 김치, 실파를 번갈아 끼운 후 한 면만 밀가루를 묻히고 달걀물에 담갔다가 빼낸다. 달군 팬에 기름을 2작은술 정도 두르고 뜨거워지면 꼬치를 놓아 노릇노릇하게 지져낸다. 돼지고기가 충분히 익도록 2~3분 정도씩 지지면 된다. 매번 팬을 깨끗이 닦고 기름을 더 넣은 후 지져야 꼬치가 깨끗하다.

sea food

Shrimp With Chili Sauce

새우 칠리소스 볶음

I have a fear of deep-frying anything. Something about the bubbling oil reminds me of medieval tales of torture with hot oil, and then I become irrationally scared that I might trip and then inadvertently "torture" myself. This presents a bit of a problem for someone who loves to cook, and loves deep-fried foods. This recipe originally called for deep-frying the shrimp, but I begged my mom to offer an alternative. I told her it was to help busy cooks save time, but we both know why I made the request. If you are more rational than me, I encourage you to try to deep-fry the shrimp, as it is a very tasty way to prepare this recipe.

Ingredients

- 1 pound large shrimp, peeled (last tail segment attached) and deveined
- 1 tablespoon rice wine • Salt and pepper • 2 tablespoons cornstarch
- ½ of a medium sized onion, chopped • 1 stalk of celery, chopped
- 2 mini red peppers, cored and seeded, chopped
- 2 jalapeño peppers or ¼ of a large green pepper, cored and seeded, chopped
- 1 clove garlic, chopped • 1 inch section of ginger, peeled and chopped
- 2 tablespoons canola oil

Ingredients for Chili Sauce

- 1 tablespoon rice wine or cooking wine • 4 tablespoons ketchup
- 2 teaspoons Sriracha chili sauce • 1 tablespoon soy sauce
- 1 tablespoon lemon juice • 1 tablespoon sugar
- 1 tablespoon sesame oil

Mix all of the ingredients for the chili sauce in a small bowl and set aside.

Marinate shrimp with rice wine, salt and black pepper for 5 minutes. Pat the shrimp very dry and place in a bowl. Toss with the cornstarch until lightly coated. Heat large frying pan over high heat. Add the cooking oil and swirl to coat. Add the cornstarch coated shrimp to the pan and spread out in one layer. Let fry untouched for 1 minute. Flip and fry the other side for another minute. Remove the shrimp from the frying pan.

Return the pan to the stove. Add an additional teaspoon of canola oil to the pan. When the pan is hot, add the garlic and the ginger. Cook for 20 seconds and add chopped vegetables. Cook for an additional minute, and then add the chili sauce, stirring to mix thoroughly. Add the cooked shrimp back into the pan, stir for about 2 minutes or until the sauce coats the shrimp and thickens. Transfer shrimp to serving dish. Garnish, if desired. Serve immediately.

재료 • 왕새우 1파운드, 꼬리는 남기고 껍질과 내장을 제거한다 • 청주 1큰술 • 소금, 후추 약간 • 감자전분 2큰술 • 양파 ½개, 잘게 썬다 • 셀러리 1줄기, 잘게 썬다 • 홍파프리카 2개, 씨를 빼고 잘게 썬다 • 청피망 ½개 또는 청고추 2개, 씨를 빼고 잘게 썬다 • 마늘 1개, 잘게 다진다 • 생강 1조각, 잘게 다진다 소스 재료 • 청주 1큰술 • 케첩 4큰술 • 칠리소스 2작은술 • 간장 1큰술 • 레몬즙 1큰술 • 설탕 1큰술 • 참기름 1큰술 소스 재료를 잘 섞어둔다.

손질해둔 새우에 청주를 뿌리고 소금과 후추로 간하여 5분간 잰 후 물기를 닦고 감자전분을 무친다. 달군 팬에 기름을 넉넉히 두르고 전분을 무친 새우를 놓아 1분간 익힌 후 뒤집어 다시 1분간 놓아둔다. 새우의 겉이 바삭하게 익으면 꺼내 접시에 담아둔다. 다시 팬을 달구어 기름을 1큰술 더 넣고 다진 생강과 마늘을 넣어 20초 정도 볶은 후 준비해둔 채소를 넣어 한 번 더 볶아준다. 거기에 섞어놓은 소스를 부어 볶다가 새우를 넣어 다시 한 번 잘 볶아내어 접시에 담아낸다.

Shrimp Stuffed Tofu 새우 두부찜

This shrimp stuffed tofu is similar to a delicious dimsum dish composed of fried eggplant stuffed with a shrimp filling. My mom wanted to create a healthier version with similar flavors, and as a favor to an eggplant-hating friend, she came up with using tofu as an alternative to the eggplant. The resulting dish is not only healthy, but also flavorful and filling.

Ingredients

- I pound firm tofu, cut into 2 inch by 2 ½ inch pieces
- 10 medium shrimp shelled, deveined, and chopped
- ½ cup of chopped chicken breast
- 2 dried shitake mushrooms, soaked in warm water
  to reconstitute for 30 minutes, stems discarded, and chopped
- 2 mini red bell peppers, chopped • 2 green chilies, chopped
- I tablespoon cornstarch • I tablespoon rice wine
- ½ teaspoon salt • ¼ teaspoon black pepper
- I tablespoon sesame oil • Vegetable oil

Ingredients for Sauce

- I cup chicken broth • I tablespoon cornstarch
- I tablespoon water • I tablespoon oyster sauce
- I teaspoon soy sauce • I teaspoon canola oil

Sprinkle salt over the sliced tofu. Heat I tablespoon of vegetable oil in a large frying pan over medium heat. Cook tofu on one side until golden brown, about 3 minutes, and remove from the pan, leaving one side uncooked. Repeat until all the pieces of tofu are browned on one side. Scoop out about a half of a tablespoon of tofu from the uncooked side of each piece and set aside in a large bowl. Add shrimp, chicken, shitake mushrooms, red pepper and green pepper to the tofu pieces. Combine the rice wine, sesame oil, salt, black pepper, and cornstarch and add to the bowl, mixing well.

Place about a tablespoon of the shrimp mixture into the hollows of each piece of tofu. Repeat with the rest of the tofu and shrimp mixture. Place the stuffed tofu into a wire basket steamer. Steam for about 10 minutes or until the shrimp filling turns pink and is done.

Combine chicken broth, oyster sauce, soy sauce, and sesame oil in a small saucepan and bring to a boil, stirring constantly. Dissolve cornstarch into I tablespoon of cold water and add to the sauce. Stir constantly to allow the sauce to thicken.

Drizzle the sauce over the steamed tofu and garnish with red pepper slices. Serve warm. Makes two servings.

재료 • 두부 한 모, 2×2.5인치 크기로 썬다 • 새우 중간 크기 10마리, 껍질과 내장을 제거하고 잘게 썬다 • 다진 닭가슴살 ½컵 • 마른 표고버섯 2장, 미지근한 물에 30분간 불려 기둥을 떼고 잘게 썬다 • 홍고추 2개 또는 파프리카, 씨를 빼고 잘게 썬다 • 청고추 2개, 씨를 빼고 잘게 썬다 • 전분 1큰술 • 맛술 1큰술 • 소금 ½작은술 • 후추 ¼작은술 • 참기름 1큰술 • 식용유(부침용) 소스 재료 • 닭육수 1컵 • 전분 1큰술 + 물 1큰술, 잘 섞는다 • 굴소스 1큰술 • 간장 1작은술 • 카놀라유 1작은술

준비해둔 두부에 소금을 살짝 뿌려둔다. 달군 팬에 기름을 두르고 두부를 한 면만 노릇하게 3분 정도 지져서 식힌 후 지지지 않은 면을 ½큰술 정도 파서 컵을 만든다. 큰 그릇에 새우, 닭가슴살, 표고버섯, 파낸 두부, 청홍고추를 넣고 맛술, 참기름, 소금, 후추를 넣어 간을 한 후 녹말가루를 넣어 잘 섞어 소를 만들어둔다. 두부에 소를 1큰술 정도씩 채우고 찜통에 얹어 속이 익을 때까지 약 10분간 쪄낸다. 작은 냄비를 불에 올려 소스 재료들을 넣고 저으면서 끓이다가 끓기 시작하면 녹말물을 넣어 꺼룩하게 만든다. 쪄낸 두부 위에 소스를 끼얹고 홍고추로 장식하여 뜨거울 때 낸다.

Pan-Fried Noodles with Seafood and Vegetables 해물 팬 프라이드 누들

My family loves this Chinese dish and wanted to create it at home. While my mom loves to use thicker noodles, the thinner egg noodles used in this recipe are my absolute favorite kind of Chinese noodles. Pan-frying them creates a nice crispy, golden crust that provides a delicious base for the warm seafood and savory sauce.

Ingredients

- ½ pound Chinese egg noodles
- 16 large shrimp, peeled, deveined and butterflied
- ½ pound large sea scallops, rinsed and sliced lengthwise into ⅓ inch slices
- 6 baby corn, quartered • ½ red bell pepper, cut into bite sized pieces
- 3 dried shitake mushrooms, soaked in warm water
  to reconstitute for 30 minutes, stems discarded and cut into strips
- 2 bunches baby bok choy, washed and cut into slices diagonally
- 3 leaves, napa cabbage, cut into bite size pieces
- 1 cup broccoli • 1 cup snow peas, trimmed • 1 teaspoon cornstarch
- ½ teaspoon salt • ¼ teaspoon pepper • Canola Oil

Ingredients for Sauce

- 1 ½ cup chicken broth • 1 tablespoon rice wine • 1 teaspoon garlic cloves, chopped
- 1 teaspoon ginger, minced • 2 teaspoons cornstarch + 1 tablespoon water
- 2 tablespoons oyster sauce • 1 tablespoon soy sauce

In a large saucepan, add enough water to cover the noodles and bring to a boil. Cook until the noodles are tender, but still firm. Rinse with cold water, draining well.

Heat a large greased skillet over medium heat, add the noodles and spread them out to the edges of the pan. Cook without stirring until browned on the bottom, about 5 minutes. Flip over and brown the other side. Remove to a plate.

Mix prepared seafood with the cornstarch, salt, and pepper and refrigerate for 5 minutes. Heat 2 tablespoons of canola oil in a frying pan over medium high heat, add garlic and ginger and saute for 10 seconds. Add seafood and cook until the shrimp turns pink. Remove and set aside.

Heat 2 tablespoons of canola oil in a separate frying pan over medium high heat. Add the vegetables and quickly sauté for a few minutes. In a separate pan, add chicken stock, rice wine, soy sauce, oyster sauce, salt, and pepper, bring to a boil, then add vegetables and seafood. Dissolve cornstarch into 1 tablespoon of cold water and add to the sauce. Stir constantly to allow the sauce to thicken. Place noodles on serving plate, and top with vegetables and seafood. Serve warm.

재료 • 중국식 에그 누들 ½파운드 • 큰 새우 16개, 껍질과 내장을 제거하고 등을 가른다 • 큰 관자 ½파운드, 씻어 물기를 빼고 ⅓인치로 저며둔다 • 베이비콘 6개, 길게 4등분해둔다 • 홍피망 ½개, 먹기 좋은 크기로 썬다 • 말린 표고버섯 3장, 미지근한 물에 30분간 불려 기둥을 떼고 채 썬다 • 청경채 2송이, 잎을 떼어 씻어서 피망과 같은 크기로 썬다 • 배춧잎 3장, 청경채와 같은 크기로 썬다 • 브로콜리 1컵 • 스노피 1컵, 끝을 다듬는다 • 전분 1작은술 • 소금 ½작은술 • 후추 ¼작은술 • 카놀라유 소스 재료 • 닭육수 1½컵 • 청주 1큰술 • 다진 마늘 1작은술 • 다진 생강 1작은술 • 전분 2작은술 + 물 1큰술 • 굴소스 2큰술 • 간장 1큰술

큰 냄비에 국수가 잠길 정도의 물을 붓고 끓으면 국수를 넣어 살짝 삶아서 찬물에 헹궈 물기를 빼둔다. 달군 팬에 기름을 두르고 물기를 뺀 국수를 펴서 겉이 파삭하게 튀겨준다. 한 번 뒤집어 노릇노릇해질 때까지 튀겨 접시에 담아둔다. 준비해둔 해물에 전분, 소금, 후추로 밑간을 해서 5분 정도 냉장보관한다. 팬을 뜨겁게 달구어 카놀라유를 2큰술 두른 후 다진 마늘과 생강으로 향을 내고 밑간해둔 해물을 넣어 새우가 분홍색으로 변할 때까지 볶아준다. 다시 팬을 달구어 카놀라유를 2큰술 두르고 준비해둔 채소들을 살짝 볶아낸다. 큰 팬에 닭육수와 맛술, 간장, 굴소스를 넣고 끓기 시작하면 볶은 채소와 해물을 넣고 녹말물을 넣어 잘 섞는다. 국물이 꺼룩해지면 큰 접시에 튀긴 누들을 놓고 그 위에 해물 채소 소스를 얹어 따뜻하게 낸다.

Iceberg Lettuce With Pan-Fried Shrimp 새우 양상추 샐러드

Iceberg lettuce is probably not the most popular choice for a salad, but it works perfectly with spicy shrimp, balancing the heat with its cool, refreshing crispness. Do not make the same mistake I did, and take too many shortcuts with this recipe. More specifically, I made this recipe using frozen boiled shrimp, and the texture of the shrimp made for an unappetizing meal. The crispness of the pan-fried shrimp is essential to this dish.

Ingredients

- 1 pound large shrimp, peeled (last tail segment attached) and deveined
- 1 tablespoon rice wine • Salt and pepper
- 2 tablespoons cornstarch • ½ of medium head iceberg lettuce, cored and shredded
- 2 red radishes, thinly sliced • Canola oil

Ingredients for Sauce

- 1 green onion (white only), chopped • 1 mini red pepper, cored and seeded, chopped
- 1 chili pepper, cored and seeded, chopped • 2 tablespoons soy sauce
- 2 tablespoons rice vinegar • 1 tablespoon sugar
- 1 tablespoon sesame oil • 2 tablespoons water

Mix all of the ingredients for the sauce until well combined and set aside.

Pour rice wine, salt and pepper over the shrimp and let marinate for 5 minutes. Pat the shrimp very dry and place in a bowl. Toss with the cornstarch until lightly coated. Heat large frying pan over high heat. Add the canola oil and swirl to coat. Add the cornstarch coated shrimp to the pan and spread out in one layer. Let fry untouched for 1 minute. Flip and fry other side for another minute. Remove the shrimp from the frying pan. Arrange the lettuce and red radishes on a serving dish and add the cooked shrimp. Pour the sauce over and serve. Garnish, if desired.

Serves 4 for appetizers, or 2 for a large dinner or lunch.

재료 • 왕새우 1파운드, 꼬리는 남기고 껍질과 내장을 제거한다 • 청주 1큰술 • 소금, 후추 약간 • 전분 2큰술 • 양상추 ½개, 잘게 뜯는다 • 래디시 2개, 얇게 썬다 • 카놀라유 소스 재료 • 파 흰 부분 1대, 다진다 • 홍파프리카 1개, 씨를 빼고 잘게 썬다 • 풋고추 1개, 씨를 빼고 잘게 썬다 • 간장 2큰술 • 식초 2큰술 • 설탕 1큰술 • 참기름 1큰술 • 물 2큰술 소스 재료를 잘 섞어둔다.

손질해둔 새우에 청주를 뿌리고 소금과 후추로 간하여 5분간 잰 후 물기를 닦고 전분을 무친다. 달군 팬에 기름을 넉넉히 두르고 전분을 무친 새우를 넣어 1분간 익힌 후 뒤집어 다시 1분간 익힌다. 새우의 겉이 바삭하게 익으면 꺼내 접시에 올려둔다. 접시에 준비해둔 양상추를 깔고 래디시로 장식한 후 새우를 얹고 소스를 뿌려낸다.

Vietnamese Spring Rolls 월남쌈

I often find the Vietnamese spring rolls served in restaurants to be bland and unimpressive. However, as is often the truth, food tastes better when you make it yourself at home. After following this recipe, I find myself loving Vietnamese spring rolls and wanting to eat them at least once a week. The rolls are fresh and bright and are perfect for a light lunch.

Ingredients
- 12 round rice paper sheets, 9 inches in diameter • 2 ounces dried vermicelli noodles
- 1 cup fresh cilantro • ½ cup mung bean sprouts, washed • 1 carrot, peeled and cut into thin strips
- 1 avocado, peeled, pitted and sliced into ¼-½ inch strips (optional)
- 5 imitation crab sticks, cut into matchstick-size strips
- 16 large shrimp, cooked, peeled and deveined, cut lengthwise in half
- ½ of a red bell pepper, cut into very thin strips
- ½ of a yellow bell pepper, cut into very thin strips
- 1 onion, thinly sliced + 3 tablespoons basic sauce,
  soak thinly sliced onion in basic sauce and set aside
- 1 cup red cabbage, julienned • 3 tablespoons basic sauce

Ingredients for Dipping Sauce:
- 2 tablespoons fermented fish sauce • 1 tablespoon fresh lemon juice
- 2 tablespoons basic sauce (Basic sauce is made of 5 parts vinegar to 4 parts sugar to 1 part salt.)
- 1 tablespoon jalapeño pepper, minced • 1 tablespoon red pepper, minced
- Mix all of the ingredients for dipping sauce until well combined and set aside.
  Let stand at least 30 minutes. (Can be made 1 day ahead. Cover and chill.)

Cook rice vermicelli according to the instructions on the package and rinse with cold water, draining well. Fill a large shallow bowl with warm water. Dip one rice paper sheet into the warm water for two seconds and turn over to moisten the other side. Soak until the paper begins to soften, then remove from the water and drain well. Lay wrapper on a flat, clean surface. In a row across the center, place 3 shrimp halves, a handful of vermicelli, and several of the prepared vegetables, leaving about 2 inches uncovered on each side. Fold uncovered sides inward, then tightly roll the wrapper around the fillings. Place rolls, seam side down on a serving platter. Repeat with remaining ingredients. Serve rice paper rolls with the dipping sauce. Serves Four.

재료(4인분) • 둥근 라이스 페이퍼(9인치) 12장 • 마른 쌀국수 2온스 • 고수 1컵 • 숙주 ½컵, 다듬어 씻는다 • 당근 1개, 껍질을 벗기고 채 썬다 • 게살 5 개, 길게 뜯어놓는다 • 큰 새우 16마리, 내장을 제거하고 익혀서 껍질을 벗겨 반으로 갈라둔다 • 홍피망 ½개, 씨를 제거하고 길고 가늘게 썬다 • 노랑 피망 ½개, 씨를 제거하고 길고 가늘게 썬다 • 양파 1개 + 베이식 소스 3큰술, 껍질을 벗기고 채 썰어 베이식 소스에 재워둔다 • 붉은 양배추 1컵, 가늘 게 채 썬다 • (선택) 아보카도 1개, 껍질과 씨를 제거하고 길고 가늘게 썬다 소스 재료 • 액젓 2큰술 • 레몬즙 1큰술 • 베이식 소스 2큰술(식초5 : 설탕4 : 소금1) • 다진 청양고추 1큰술 • 다진 홍고추 1큰술 재료를 잘 섞어 30분 정도 둔다. 하루 전에 만들어 냉장고에 넣어두어도 좋다.

쌀국수는 끓는 물에 3분간 삶아서 찬물에 헹궈 물기를 빼둔다. 라이스 페이퍼를 따뜻한 물에 한 장씩 2초 정도 담가 부드러워지 면 건져 물기를 뺀다. 반 가른 새우를 3개 깔고 그 위에 준비해둔 재료들을 넣고 양 옆을 접어 원통으로 말아준다. 접시에 담고 소 스와 함께 낸다.

Okonomiyaki (Japanese Savory Pancake) 오코노미야키

Okonomiyaki is a Japanese street food. The word "okonomi" means, "what you like" or "what you want" and "yaki" means, "grilled" or "cooked." Okonomiyaki is a cabbage pancake that is very adaptable. You can add different flavorings to the batter, or choose from several different toppings, hence the "okonomi" part of the name. The pancakes are often grilled or cooked in a frying pan, hence the "yaki" part of the name. Thus, Okonomiyaki are cabbage pancakes with the addition of whatever you like, that are grilled or pan-fried.

Ingredients
• ½ cup nagaimo, peeled and grated
  (if you are unable to find nagaimo, you can replace it with ¼ cup flour + 1 egg)
• ¼ cup all purpose flour, sifted
• ¼ cup dashi water (water with a pinch of dashi powder) or just water
• 2 eggs • 6 shrimp, peeled and cut into small pieces
• 2 cups roughly chopped cabbage • 6 to 8 pieces of bacon or thinly sliced pork
• 3 tablespoons green onion, chopped • Canola oil for cooking

Toppings
• ¼ cup katsuobushi (dried bonito flakes)
• 3 tablespoons mayonnaise + 1 teaspoon wasabi (optional), mixed well
• 3 tablespoons okonomiyaki sauce or tonkatsu sauce

Mix nagaimo with the dashi water, flour and eggs in a large bowl. The batter should be loose. Add the cabbage, green onion and shrimp to the batter and combine.

Heat a large frying pan over medium heat and add about 2 tablespoons of vegetable oil. When the oil is hot, spread ⅓ of the batter in a circle in the pan. Place 2 to 3 strips of pork or bacon as flat as possible on top of the batter. Cover the frying pan and let the okonomiyaki steam for about 5-6 minutes. When the pork has lightened up in color, or the bacon looks cooked, flip the okonomiyaki. Continue cooking without a lid for about 3 more minutes. Lower the heat and press down on the okonomiyaki squeeze some air and fluffiness out. Flip the okonomiyaki again and place on a serving platter. Repeat with the rest of the batter. To eat, spread okonomiyaki sauce and mayonnaise on top.

Optional: sprinkle katsuobushi on top as well. Makes two or three servings.

재료(2~3인분) • 간 마 ½컵(또는 밀가루 ¼컵 + 달걀 1개) • 밀가루 ¼컵 • 다시 국물(또는 물) ¼컵 • 달걀 2개 • 새우 6개, 껍질을 벗기고 잘게 썬다 • 양배추 2컵, 잘게 썬다 • 베이컨(또는 삼겹살) 6~8줄 • 잘게 썬 파 3큰술 • 카놀라유(부침용) 토핑 재료 • 가쓰오부시 ¼컵 • 마요네즈 3큰술 + 와사비 1작은술, 잘 섞는다 • 오코노미야키 소스(또는 돈가스 소스) 3큰술

마는 껍질을 벗기고 갈아서 다시 국물, 밀가루, 달걀과 같이 섞고 잘게 썰어놓은 양배추, 파, 새우를 넣어 반죽을 만든다. 달군 팬에 기름을 2큰술 두르고 반죽의 ⅓을 넣고 둥글게 펴준 다음 베이컨(또는 삼겹살)을 2~3줄 위에 얹는다. 뚜껑을 덮고 5~6분 가량 지져 돼지고기가 익으면 뚜껑을 열고 뒤집어 위를 눌러 공기를 빼주면서 3분 정도 더 익힌다. 오코노미야키가 다 되면 소스와 마요네즈를 위에 바르고 가쓰오부시를 원하는 만큼 올려서 낸다.

tip 다시 국물이 없으면 물에 다시 가루를 조금 넣어도 좋다.

Yama Imo

127

Potato Rolled Shrimp Tempura 새우 감자말이 튀김

The inspiration for this recipe comes from a dish my mom had at a restaurant in Korea. Instead of serving a traditional shrimp tempura, which is battered and fried, this restaurant rolled the shrimp in noodles and fried them, replacing the batter with a fried coating of noodles. This recipe borrows the same technique, but substitutes thin, crisply fried potatoes for the noodles. The potato turns into a French fry like coating that is part potato pancake, part shrimp tempura.

Ingredients

- 10 large shrimp, shelled and deveined, leaving tail intact
- 1 tablespoon rice wine • 1 medium potato, peeled and shredded
- 2 ounces sweet potato noodles • 2 tablespoons cornstarch
- ⅓ cup all purpose flour • ¼ teaspoon salt
- ⅛ teaspoon black pepper • Canola oil for frying

Ingredients for Tempura Sauce

- ¼ cup soy sauce • ¼ cup rice wine
- 1 cup dashi broth (2 inches kombu + 2 tablespoons bonito flakes)
- 1 tablespoon daikon radish, grated • 1 tablespoon green onion, chopped

Put two cups of cold water in a medium saucepan. Wipe down kombu with a damp paper towel and soak it in the water for about 30 minutes. Take kombu out, add bonito flakes and leave for 5 minutes and strain. Put the liquid back into the pot and add soy sauce and rice wine. Bring to a boil and then remove from heat. Add grated daikon radish and chopped onion to the tempura sauce just before serving.

Make two or three incisions on the stomach side of the shrimp to straighten them. Lightly press the back of shrimp until they form a straight line. Using a knife, remove the dirt from the tails of shrimp. Sprinkle rice wine on shrimp. Rinse shredded potatoes in a large bowl of cold water and drain well. In a small bowl, combine the shredded potato with cornstarch. Combine flour, salt, and pepper in a separate bowl. Dry shrimp with paper towel and dredge in flour mixture until all surfaces are lightly covered. Take a small portion of the potato mixture and roll it around a shrimp until it surrounds it completely. Repeat with the rest of the potato mixture and shrimp and set aside.

Heat oil in a deep frying pan over high heat to 350 F. Fry sweet potato noodles until crisp. Drain well on a paper towel. Slip potato rolled shrimp into deep oil and fry until crisp and golden brown. Drain well on a paper towel. Put the fried noodles onto a serving plate. Arrange the shrimp on top of the noodles. Serve with tempura sauce.

재료(2~3인분) • 새우 10마리, 꼬리는 붙여두고 껍질과 내장을 제거한다 • 청주 1큰술 • 감자 1개, 껍질을 벗기고 채 썰어 찬물에 헹궈 물기를 뺀다 • 녹말가루 2큰술 • 밀가루 ⅓컵 • 당면 2온스 • 소금 ¼작은술 • 후추 ⅛작은술 • 카놀라유(튀김용) 튀김장 재료 • 간장 ¼컵 • 청주 ¼컵 • 다시마물 1컵 (사방 4센티 다시마 + 가쓰오부시 2큰술) • 무즙 1큰술 • 송송 썬 실파 1큰술

미지근한 물에 다시마를 30분 정도 불렸으다가 꺼내고 가쓰오부시를 넣어 5분간 두었다 체에 걸러낸다. 팬에 간장과 청주를 섞어 한번 끓으면 다시마물을 섞고 불을 끈다. 강판에 간 무와 송송 썬 파를 만들어놓은 튀김 간장에 얹어낸다. 새우는 꼬리 부분의 물주머니를 떼어낸 다음 배 부분에 세 번 칼집을 내고 살짝 잡아당겨 곧게 펴준다. 새우에 청주를 뿌려 밑간을 한다. 감자를 물이 담긴 볼에 제일 가는 채칼로 채를 썰어 물기를 짜서 전분을 묻혀둔다. 밑간해둔 새우의 물기를 종이타월로 닦고 밀가루를 얇게 묻혀 준비해둔 감자채로 돌돌 말아둔다. 깊은 팬에 카놀라유를 넣고 기름이 뜨거워지면 먼저 당면을 짧게 잘라 튀겨 기름을 빼둔다. 감자채에 말아둔 새우를 넣어 노릇하게 튀겨지면 바로 건져 기름기를 뺀다. 당면을 접시에 깔고 위에 새우 감자말이 튀김을 얹어 장식해낸다.

Soy Sauce Cod
with Sautéed Vegetables 간장 소스를 곁들인 대구와 채소볶음

Growing up, fish was a fixture at our house for dinner. For some reason, when I learned to cook, I usually dealt with chicken or beef but neglected to learn how to cook fish. Eventually, I began to miss having fish regularly, but would have no idea how to cook it. This recipe is perfect for people who do not have a lot of experience cooking fish. It is easy, quick and surprisingly impressive for a minimal amount of work.

Ingredients

• 1 pound cod, cut into 4 inch pieces • 2 tablespoons flour
• ¼ teaspoon salt • ⅛ teaspoon black pepper
• ¼ large onion, cut into ½ inch cubes • ½ cup steamed broccoli
• ½ red bell pepper, cut into ½ inch cubes • 2 tablespoons canola oil

Ingredients for Sauce

• 2 tablespoons soy sauce • 1 tablespoon rice wine
• 1 ½ tablespoons sugar • 2 cloves garlic, thinly sliced
• 1 tablespoon sesame oil • ¼ teaspoon black pepper

Mix together all ingredients for sauce and set aside. Season the cod with salt and pepper and then lightly dust with flour. Heat a large frying pan over medium high heat and add 1 tablespoon of canola oil. Add chopped vegetables to the pan and sauté until softened.

Put sauce ingredients into a small saucepan and bring to a boil. Continue to boil until bubbly and the sauce is thickened. Heat 1 tablespoon of canola oil in a large frying pan over high heat and add the cod. Cook the cod until evenly browned and crispy, about 2 minutes per side. Remove from pan. Place cod on a serving plate with vegetables on top. Pour sauce over cod and vegetables to taste.

재료 • 대구 1파운드, 4인치 길이로 토막을 낸다 • 밀가루 2큰술 • 소금 ¼작은술 • 후추 ⅛작은술 • 큰 양파 ¼개, 잘게 썬다 • 데친 브로콜리 ½컵, 잘게 썬다 • 홍피망 ½개, 잘게 썬다 • 카놀라유 2큰술 소스 재료 • 간장 2큰술 • 청주 1큰술 • 설탕 1 ½큰술 • 마늘 2개, 얇게 저며 썬다 • 참기름 1큰술 • 후추 ¼작은술 소스 재료를 잘 섞어놓는다.

대구에 소금과 후추로 밑간을 하고 겉에 밀가루를 살짝 묻힌다. 달군 팬에 기름을 1큰술 두르고 썰어놓은 양파와 홍피망, 브로콜리를 넣고 색이 살도록 살짝 볶아낸다. 작은 냄비에 소스 재료를 넣어 거품이 날 때까지 끓인다. 프라이팬을 달구어 기름을 1큰술 두르고 준비해둔 대구를 겉이 파삭하게 지진 다음 뒤집어서 약 2분 정도 더 지진다. 접시에 지진 대구를 담고 볶은 채소를 위에 얹은 후 끓여둔 간장 소스를 뿌려낸다.

Sake-Steamed Seafood and Vegetables 정종에 데친 해물채소찜

A few years ago I had the opportunity to go on a tour of Northern Japan with my mother and grandmother. One of our stops was in Sapporo, where we had a delicious meal of steamed seafood, udon noodles, and vegetables. We absolutely loved it, but the other members of our group complained that it lacked flavor. When our vacation was over, my mom decided to add sea salt and sake in order to enhance the flavors of the ingredients without overpowering them. She also added a dipping sauce in case the flavors are a bit too subtle for your personal taste, but the dish is also wonderful without it.

Ingredients

• ½ pound large shrimp • ½ pound sea scallops
• I pound mussels • I pound broccoli florets, cut into small pieces
• I bunch of enoki mushrooms, with the bottoms trimmed
• ¼ pound bacon, cut into 2 inch pieces • I package frozen udon noodles
• ¼ cup of sake • ¼ teaspoon sea salt • I clove garlic, thinly sliced
• ½ pound okra, cut into small pieces

Ingredients for Dipping Sauce

• 2 tablespoons soy sauce • I scallion, chopped
• I clove of garlic, minced • I teaspoon toasted sesame seeds
• I tablespoon sugar • I tablespoon rice vinegar • I teaspoon sesame oil

Mix together all ingredients for Dipping Sauce and set aside. Blanch broccoli and okra slightly in boiling water. Put prepared vegetables, bacon, udon noodles and seafood into a large frying pan over high heat. Add sake, sliced garlic and salt. Cover the pan with a lid and cook until the shrimp turns pink and the mussels open. Serve immediately with or without dipping sauce. Serves 2.

재료(2인분) • 큰 새우 ½파운드 • 관자 ½파운드 • 홍합 1파운드 • 브로콜리 1파운드, 먹기 좋은 크기로 잘라 데친다 • 팽이버섯 1봉지, 밑동을 자르고 뜯어둔다 • 베이컨 ¼파운드, 2인치 크기로 썰어둔다 • 생우동 국수(사누키 우동 국수 얼린 것) 1팩, 꺼내서 녹인다 • 정종 ¼컵 • 바다소금 ¼작은술 • 마늘 1개, 얇게 썬다 • 오크라 ½파운드, 살짝 데쳐 어슷하게 반으로 썰어둔다 디핑 소스 • 간장 2큰술 • 다진 파 1큰술 • 다진 마늘 1작은술 • 볶은 깨 1 작은술 • 설탕 1큰술 • 식초 1큰술 • 참기름 1작은술 소스 재료를 잘 섞어둔다.

준비해둔 채소와 해물, 베이컨, 버섯과 우동 국수를 전골냄비에 보기 좋게 얹은 후 정종, 썰어놓은 마늘과 소금을 위에 뿌린다. (삶지 않은 국수를 생우동 국수로 사용할 때는 삶아서 물기를 뺀 후 사용한다.) 뚜껑을 덮고 새우가 분홍색으로 변할 때까지 약 5분간 끓여 디핑 소스와 함께 낸다. 디핑 소스가 없어도 간이 잘 맞고 맛이 깔끔하다.

Spicy Stir-Fried Octopus (Nakjibokum) 낙지볶음

Spicy Stir-Fried Octopus, or Nakjibokum is typically served with rice or noodles, which are mixed with the sauce. It is often brought to the table in an electric skillet, which ensures that it is served piping hot. This dish is definitely for people who love spicy food and is the perfect accompaniment to ice-cold sake or soju.

Ingredients

• 1 pound raw octopus (or squid if octopus is not available)
• ½ onion, cut into thin strips • 2 green onions, cut into 2 inch pieces
• 2 green chili peppers, sliced on the bias • 2 red chili peppers, sliced on the bias
• 2 cabbage leaves, cut into pieces • 1 bunch of enoki mushrooms, with bottoms trimmed
• 2 bunches baby bok choy, washed with stalks and leaves separated • 2 tablespoons canola oil

Ingredients for Sauce

• 2 tablespoons Korean hot pepper paste (gochujang) • 2 tablespoons ground red pepper
• 1 tablespoon rice wine • 2 tablespoons soy sauce • 1 ½ tablespoons sugar
• 2 teaspoons toasted sesame seeds • 1 tablespoon sesame oil • 1 tablespoon garlic, minced

Mix all ingredients for sauce except sesame oil and sesame seeds and set aside. Place trimmed and cleaned bok choy into a vegetable steamer and steam for 5 minutes. Rinse with ice water and drain well set aside. Wash octopus in cold, salted water, open the heads and take out innards. Quarter the heads and drain octopus well. Bring a large pot of water to a boil. Add octopus and cook for about 3 minutes. Drain and cut the legs into 2-3″ lengths. Pour prepared sauce over the octopus and mix until well coated and set aside.

Heat canola oil in a large frying pan over medium heat, add vegetables and stir-fry for 2 minutes. Add octopus and cook for 2 more minutes, then add sesame oil and mix again to coat. Garnish with steamed baby bok choy and toasted sesame seeds.

재료 • 낙지 2마리(1파운드) • 양파 ½개, 굵게 채 썬다 • 파 2뿌리, 2인치 길이로 썬다 • 청홍고추 2개씩, 어슷하게 썬다 • 양배추잎 2개, 다른 채소와 같은 크기로 썬다 • 팽이버섯 1봉지, 밑동을 자른다 • 청경채 2개, 뜯어서 깨끗이 씻는다 • 카놀라유 2큰술 양념장 재료 • 고추장 2큰술 • 고춧가루 2 큰술 • 청주 1큰술 • 간장 2큰술 • 설탕 1 ½큰술 • 볶은 깨 2작은술 • 참기름 1큰술 • 다진 마늘 1큰술

참기름과 볶은 깨를 뺀 나머지 양념 재료들을 잘 섞어둔다. 청경채는 살짝 데쳐 찬물에 헹궈 물기를 빼놓고, 낙지는 머리를 뒤집어 내장을 제거하고 먹물을 떼어낸 뒤 굵은 소금으로 거품이 나도록 주물러 닦아 깨끗이 헹구어 물기를 빼둔다. 끓는 물에 낙지를 살짝 데쳐 찬물에 헹궈서 한입 크기(6센티)로 잘라 섞어둔 양념으로 버무린다. 달군 팬에 기름을 두르고 채소를 넣어 볶다가 어느 정도 익으면 낙지를 넣고 센 불에서 재빨리 볶은 다음 마지막으로 참기름을 두르고 깨를 뿌려준다. 접시에 청경채를 깔고 낙지볶음을 소복하게 담아내거나 적당한 크기로 썰어 예쁘게 곁들여낸다.

Seafood Dukboki 해물떡볶이

There are many different varieties of dukboki. Spicy dukboki made with ricecakes and fishcakes, or sometimes a non-spicy version made with marinated beef. This version adds seafood and vegetables, making a more balanced meal and lightening up the starch heavy dish.

Ingredients

• 1 pound rice cakes, cut into 2 inch pieces
• 3 leaves red cabbage, cut into 1 × 2 inch pieces • ½ carrot, cut into thin strips
• 2 red mini bell peppers or ½ red bell pepper, cut into bite sized pieces
• 2 bunches baby bok choy, washed and cut into 2 inch pieces
• 1 large squid (without the legs, body only), cleaned and cut into ½ inch rings
• 10 mussels, scrubbed and beards removed
• 10 large shrimp, peeled and deveined • 2 green onions, chopped
• 1 cup seafood broth or water reserved after cooking the seafood

Ingredients for Sauce

• 3 tablespoons gochujang (Korean hot pepper paste) • 1 tablespoon rice wine
• 2 tablespoons soy sauce • 1 tablespoon fish sauce
• 1 tablespoon sugar • 2 teaspoons toasted sesame seeds
• 1 tablespoon sesame oil • 1 tablespoon garlic, minced

Combine all of the ingredients for the sauce and mix well. Bring a medium sized pot of water to a boil. Add squid, mussels, and shrimp, cooking until the squid just begins to curl, the shrimp is pink, and the mussels open. Remove the seafood from the pot and reserve the resulting broth.

Heat 1 tablespoon of canola oil in a large frying pan over medium high heat. Add vegetables and sauté until softened. Add seafood broth and sauce, bring to a boil and add ricecakes. Carefully fold the sauce and vegetables over the ricecakes until they are soft. Add seafood and mix until well coated. Garnish with sesame seeds and chopped green onion. Serve warm.

재료 • 떡볶이용 떡 1파운드, 2인치 크기로 썰어둔다 • 적양배추 3장, 1×2인치 크기로 썬다 • 당근 ½개, 양배추와 비슷한 크기로 얇게 썬다 • 홍파프리카 2개 또는 홍피망 ½개, 씨를 빼고 다른 채소와 같은 크기로 썬다 • 청경채 2개, 뜯어서 깨끗이 씻어 준비한다 • 오징어(몸통) 1개, 껍질과 내장을 제거하고 링으로 0.5인치 두께로 썬다 • 홍합 10개, 수염을 제거하고 깨끗이 씻어 물기를 뺀다 • 새우 10개, 껍질과 내장을 제거한다 • 실파 2뿌리, 송송 썬다 • 해물 데친 육수 1컵 양념장 재료 • 고추장 3큰술 • 청주 1큰술 • 간장 2큰술 • 액젓 1큰술 • 설탕 1큰술 • 볶은 깨 2작은술 • 참기름 1큰술 • 다진 마늘 1큰술 육수를 뺀 양념장 재료를 잘 섞어둔다.

냄비에 물을 넣고 끓어오르면 오징어, 홍합, 새우를 넣고 살짝 데쳐 건져놓고 국물을 체에 밭쳐 깨끗이 준비해둔다. 달군 프라이팬에 기름을 두르고 준비해둔 채소를 색이 살도록 볶아내고 해물을 데친 육수와 양념장을 넣은 다음 떡을 넣어 말랑말랑해질 때까지 끓여준다. 떡이 말랑해지면 데쳐둔 해물과 채소를 넣어 살짝 함께 볶아낸다. 준비한 접시에 떡볶이를 담고 실파와 깨로 장식한다.

Sizzling Rice Soup 해물누룽지탕

One of the best parts of Sizzling Rice Soup is the fun, popping noise you hear when the crispy rice is added to the soup. It lets you know that the soup is piping hot and ready to be eaten. Whenever I hear that sizzle, my stomach starts to grumble, and all I can think about is eating those bits of crispy and chewy rice, soaked in a rich seafood soup. *Cook's Note: Crispy rice can be made in a frying pan, which is actually how my mom usually makes it. However, it is much easier to make in larger quantities in the oven and the results are much more consistent. You can also buy pre-made crispy rice at the Asian grocery store.

Ingredients

- 10 pieces crispy rice (recipe below) • 2 cups canola oil for frying
- 1 large squid (without legs, body only), cut open and cleaned
- 10 large shrimp, peeled and deveined
- ½ cup sliced bamboo shoots, cut into thin slices
- 2 dried shitake mushrooms, soaked in warm water
  to reconstitute for 30 minutes, stems discarded and cut into thick strips
- 2 heads baby bok choy, the leaves separated from the stalks, cut into 2 inch pieces
- ½ yellow bell pepper, cut into strips
- ½ bundle enoki mushrooms, with root ends trimmed
- 2 cups chicken broth • 1 tablespoon cornstarch + 1 tablespoon water
- 1 tablespoon soy sauce • 1 tablespoon rice wine
- ½ tablespoon oyster sauce • 1 tablespoon sesame oil
- 1 clove garlic, thinly sliced • 1 green onion, chopped

Using the tip of knife, score the side of the squid that curls inward in a crisscross pattern and cut into 1×2 inch pieces. Quickly sauté the squid and shrimp in a hot skillet with 1 tablespoon of canola oil. Remove and set aside.

Add 1 tablespoon of oil and sauté shitake mushrooms, bamboo shoots, enoki mushrooms and yellow bell peppers over high heat until softened.

In a clean skillet, heat 1 tablespoon of canola oil over medium high heat. Add garlic and green onion and stir-fry for 10 seconds. Add seafood and vegetables and cook for 30 more seconds. Add soy sauce, rice wine, oyster sauce and chicken broth, and bring to a boil. Reduce the heat and stir in cornstarch mixture and sesame oil to taste.

Heat two cups of canola oil in a wok over high heat. When oil is ready, add the Crispy Rice. Deep-fry until it puffs and turns brown, then drain very briefly on paper towels.

Pour the soup into serving bowls and add the rice to the bowls at the table so that guests can hear the rice make popping sounds when added to the soup. If both are hot enough, your soup should sizzle. Makes two servings.

To Make Crispy Rice: Rinse 1 cup of short grain rice 3 or 4 times in cold water and drain. Put the rice and 1 ¼ cups of water into a rice cooker and cook according to manufacturer's directions. If you do not have a rice cooker put rice and 1 ¼ cups water in a pot and bring to a boil. Cover and simmer on low heat for 30 minutes. Remove from heat and allow to cool.

While rice is cooling, preheat oven to 300F. Place cooked rice on a baking sheet, making sure that it is about, but no more than, ¼ inch thick. Bake the rice for 50~55 minutes, until it is dry and crispy. Cool and cut into 2 inch squares.

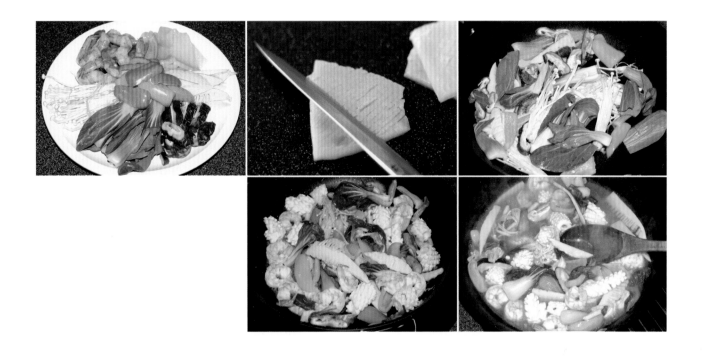

재료 • 누룽지 10조각 • 카놀라유 2컵(튀김용) • 큰 오징어(몸통) 1마리, 껍질과 내장을 제거한다 • 새우 10마리, 껍질과 내장을 제거한다 • 죽순 ½컵, 무늬가 살도록 얇게 썬다 • 마른 표고버섯 2개, 미지근한 물에 30분 정도 불려서 밑동은 자르고 두툼하게 썬다 • 청경채 2개, 씻어서 2인치 길이로 썬다 • 노랑 피망 ½개, 굵은 채로 썬다 • 팽이버섯 ½봉지, 밑동을 제거하고 몇 가닥씩 뜯어놓는다 • 닭육수 2컵 • 전분 1큰술 + 물 1큰술, 잘 풀어둔다 • 간장 1큰술 • 청주 1큰술 • 굴소스 ½큰술 • 참기름 1큰술 • 마늘 1개, 얇게 저며 썬다 • 쪽파 1대, 채 썬다

오징어는 껍질을 벗기고 가로세로로 칼집을 넣은 뒤 2×5센티 크기로 썬다. 팬에 기름을 두르고 오징어와 새우를 먼저 살짝 익혀 내고, 다시 기름을 둘러 표고버섯과 죽순, 청경채, 팽이버섯, 피망을 살짝 볶아낸다. 다시 기름을 두른 팬에 썰어둔 파와 마늘을 넣어 향이 나면 볶아둔 해물과 채소를 넣어 다시 한 번 볶아 간장과 청주, 굴소스로 간을 한 다음 육수를 붓고 끓인다. 끓으면 불을 줄이고 녹말물을 넣어 재빨리 섞은 다음 참기름을 넣어 고루 섞는다. 달궈진 카놀라유에 누룽지를 넣고 바삭하게 튀겨 종이에 올려 기름기를 뺀 다음 그릇에 담고 먹기 직전에 뜨거운 소스를 끼얹어낸다. (시판 누룽지를 사용해도 좋다.)

누룽지 만들기 쌀 1컵을 깨끗이 씻어 물 1¼컵을 넣어 밥을 짓는다. 밥이 다 되면 오븐을 300도로 예열한다. 베이킹팬에 밥을 얇게(¼인치 두께) 펴서 예열된 오븐에 넣고 50~55분간 구워 누룽지를 만든다. 식혀서 사방 2인치 크기로 잘라서 쓴다.

vegetarian

Simple Asian Slaw with Black Sesame Rice

양배추무침과 검정깨 밥

When my mom first came up with this recipe she packed it for my dad's lunch expecting complaints about the lack of meat. Surprisingly, he went absolutely crazy over the slaw and asked for the same lunch again the next day. He loved the refreshing, crisp, crunch of the slaw, and the way the nutty black sesame seeds and warm rice balanced the sourness of the dressing. The slaw and rice together form a sort of fresh vegetable bibimbap that made the perfect lunch.

Ingredients

- 2 cups green cabbage, shredded
- 1 cup red cabbage, shredded
- 1 cup sugar snap peas, steamed
  and cut diagonally into matchsticks
- 1 carrot, cut into matchsticks
- ¼ cup basic sauce (vinegar 5: sugar 4: salt 1)
- 1 tablespoon sesame oil
- 1 teaspoon toasted black sesame seeds

Ingredients for Sesame Rice

- 2 cups cooked short grain rice
- 1 tablespoon sesame oil
- ¼ teaspoon salt
- 1 teaspoon toasted black sesame seeds

Combine all of the ingredients for sesame rice and set aside.

In a small bowl, whisk together the basic sauce, sesame oil, sesame seeds to make the dressing. Combine the green and red cabbages, sugar snap peas, and carrots in a separate bowl. Add the dressing and toss to combine. Serve with black sesame rice. Makes two servings.

재료(2인분) • 채 썬 양배추 2컵 • 채 썬 적양배추 1컵 • 슈가스냅 1컵, 데쳐서 길게 썬다 • 당근 1 개, 채 썬다 소스 재료 • 베이식 소스 ¼컵(식초5 : 설탕4 : 소금1) • 참기름 1큰술 • 볶은 검정깨 1 작은술 비빔 양념 재료 • 밥 2공기 • 참기름 1큰술 • 소금 ¼작은술 • 볶은 검정깨 1작은술 볼에 밥과 참기름, 소금, 검정깨를 넣고 잘 섞어둔다.

작은 볼에 베이식 소스, 참기름, 볶은 검정깨를 넣어 섞어 소스를 만들어둔다. 볶은 검정깨, 소금, 참기름에 비벼둔 밥을 곁들여낸다.

Stir-Fried Mushrooms and Vegetables 버섯 채소볶음

My husband is not a fan of mushrooms, and unfortunately I love them. I say unfortunately because I do not want to make anything for dinner that he won't eat, so I never get to cook anything with mushrooms for dinner. So, whenever I am out to dinner with some friends or just making dinner for myself, I go a little crazy and make something extra mushroom-filled. This recipe is something I would love to eat next time I get to go a little mushroom crazy.

Ingredients

• 6 ounces mixed fresh mushrooms
• 10 asparagus, tough ends snapped off, steamed and cut in half vertically and again horizontally
• 2 cups green cabbage, shredded • ½ red bell pepper, sliced thinly
• 4 tablespoons canola oil • Salt and pepper
• 2 cups cooked brown rice or white rice (optional)

Ingredients for Dressing

• 1 tablespoon soy sauce • 2 teaspoons sugar • ½ teaspoon garlic, minced
• 2 teaspoons toasted sesame seeds • 1 tablespoon sesame oil

Mix together ingredients for dressing except sesame oil, and set aside.

Heat 2 tablespoons of canola oil in a large frying pan over medium high heat. Quickly sauté fresh mushrooms over high heat until soft, about 1 minute. Remove from pan. Add another tablespoon of canola oil. Add cabbage and red bell pepper and sauté until softened. Sprinkle with a little salt and pepper to taste.

In a large bowl, combine mushrooms, sautéed vegetables and asparagus with dressing, mixing well. Next, add sesame oil and mix again. Serve with brown or white rice. Makes two servings.

재료(2인분) • 모듬 버섯 6온스 • 아스파라거스 10개, 끝을 다듬고 살짝 데쳐서 가로, 세로로 반을 자른다 • 채 썬 양배추 2컵 • 홍피망 ½개, 채 썬다 • 카놀라유 4큰술 • 소금, 후추 약간 • (선택) 현미밥 또는 흰 쌀밥 2공기 무침 양념 재료 • 간장 1큰술 • 설탕 2작은술 • 마늘 ½작은술 • 볶은 깨 2작은술 • 참기름 1큰술 참기름을 뺀 양념 재료를 섞어둔다.

뜨겁게 달군 팬에 기름을 두르고 버섯을 넣어 센 불에 빠르게 볶아내고 기름을 1큰술 더 넣고 채 썰어둔 채소를 넣어 볶아 소금, 후추로 간을 한다. 큰 그릇에 볶은 버섯과 채소를 넣고 무침 양념을 넣어 잘 섞어준 다음 참기름을 넣어 다시 한 번 잘 섞어낸다. 큰 접시에 담고 파슬리를 장식하여 밥과 함께 낸다.

Tofu Kimchi Bibimbap 두부 김치 비빔밥

This Tofu Kimchi Bibimbop is a great meatless meal option for any vegetarians out there. When you squeeze the water out of the tofu and season it with salt, the tofu becomes almost like a drier ricotta cheese in texture and taste. While it does not have the punch of the other ingredients in the bibimbop, it does compliment them beautifully while adding a great source of protein. I would like to acknowledge that the idea to prepare tofu in this manner came from two friends of mine, whose mother often prepares bibimbap using this method. Thanks for introducing me to such a delicious and healthy way of eating tofu! *Cook's Note: Be sure to squeeze as much water as you possibly can out of the tofu, otherwise it will be too wet and make the bibimbap gummy and unpleasant to eat.

Ingredients

- 2 cups napa cabbage kimchi, finely chopped and mixed with 1 tablespoon of sesame oil
- 1 cup (½ pound) medium hard tofu
- 1 tablespoon sesame oil • ⅛ teaspoon salt
- 2 leaves of lettuce, shredded
- 2 pickling cucumbers, cut into thin strips
- 1 carrot, peeled and cut into thin strips
- 2 tablespoons canola oil
- 1 cup red cabbage, cut into thin strips
- 2 cups cooked short grain rice, mixed with 1 tablespoon of sesame oil and ¼ teaspoon of salt
- Salt

Ingredients for Sauce

- 1 ½ tablespoons gochujang (Korean hot pepper paste)
- 1 tablespoon sugar • 1 tablespoon vinegar • 1 tablespoon sesame oil
- 2 teaspoons toasted sesame seeds • ½ teaspoon garlic, minced
- 1 tablespoon green onion, minced

Mix together ingredients for sauce and set aside.

Place tofu into a cheesecloth and squeeze as much water as you can out of it. Remove the tofu from the cheesecloth and season with ⅛ teaspoon of salt. Heat 1 tablespoon of canola oil in a frying pan over high heat, and add cucumbers. Sauté for about 1 minute and sprinkle with a little salt to taste, then remove from the pan and set aside to cool. Repeat the same process with the carrot and red cabbage.

Now, heat sesame oil in the same frying pan over medium high heat and sauté seasoned tofu and kimchi separately for about 1 minute each. Put seasoned rice in two medium bowls and arrange other ingredients over the rice. Serve with sauce, allowing each person to add his or her preferred amount of sauce. Mix all of the ingredients together and eat. Makes two servings.

재료(2인분) • 채 썬 배추김치 2컵 + 참기름 1큰술 • 두부 ½파운드 + 소금 ⅛작은술, 물기를 빼고 으깨서 소금으로 간을 한다 • 참기름 1큰술 • 상추 2 잎, 채 썬다 • 피클오이 2개, 채 썬다 • 당근 1개, 껍질을 벗기고 채 썬다 • 채 썬 적양배추 1컵 • 카놀라유 2큰술 • 밥 2공기 + 참기름 1큰술 + 소금 ¼작 은술, 잘 섞어둔다 • 소금 비빔장 재료 • 고추장 1 ½큰술 • 설탕 1큰술 • 식초 1큰술 • 참기름 1큰술 • 볶은 깨 2작은술 • 다진 마늘 ½작은술 • 다진 파 1큰술 비빔장 재료들을 잘 섞어둔다.

밥에 참기름과 소금을 넣어 잘 섞어 밑간을 해둔다. 센 불로 달군 팬에 카놀라유를 1큰술 두르고 오이를 넣어 약 1분간 살짝 볶아 낸다. 팬을 닦아 다시 기름을 두르고 당근과 적양배추를 넣어 각각 숨이 죽을 때까지 볶아낸다. 다시 팬을 달궈 참기름을 두르고 준비해둔 두부와 김치를 각각 볶아 준비한다. 다른 재료를 볶을 때마다 종이타월로 팬을 닦아내고 볶아야 깔끔하다. 우묵한 볼 에 밑간해둔 밥을 나누어 담고 준비해둔 재료를 색을 맞춰 올려 비빔장과 같이 낸다.

Pan-Fried Tofu with Sweet and Sour Sauce 탕수두부

I do not often fry tofu for two main reasons: First, society has taught me to think of tofu as "healthy" and frying tofu seems counter to that. Second, fried tofu is usually spongy and unappetizing. The first reason is easily dismissed, but the second is not. This recipe, however, completely changed my mind about fried tofu. As it turns out, freshly fried tofu is completely different from stale fried tofu, and all of the fried tofu I had eaten up until that point was stale. Freshly fried tofu is crisp on the outside and almost molten on the inside. It is oddly decadent for such a "healthy" ingredient, and it pairs well with rich, slightly sweet sauces. The sweet and sour sauce in this recipe is perfect with the crisp, flavorful cubes of tofu. You can serve this dish as an appetizer, or with rice as lunch or dinner.

Ingredients

• 1 pound firm tofu, drained, rinsed and cut into 1 inch cubes
• ½ cup cornstarch • ½ cup canola oil
• 1 large leaf of green cabbage, cut into 1×2 inch pieces
• ¼ carrot, peeled and thinly sliced • ½ small cucumber, thinly sliced

Ingredients for Sweet and Sour Sauce

• 1 cup vegetable broth or water • 1 tablespoon canola oil
• 1 teaspoon garlic, chopped • 1 teaspoon ginger, chopped
• 2 tablespoons soy sauce • 5 tablespoons brown sugar • 2 tablespoons vinegar
• 1 tablespoon cornstarch + 1 tablespoon water, mixed well

Mix together all of the ingredients for the Sweet and Sour Sauce except for the cornstarch and water mixture. Put ½ cup of cornstarch in a small bowl and dredge each tofu cube until all surfaces are fully covered and set aside. Heat canola oil in a large skillet over medium heat. Add the tofu pieces and cook until each side is golden brown and crispy. Remove tofu from the pan and add vegetables. Cook for 1 minute and remove from the pan.

Heat a small thick-bottomed pot over high heat. Add the sauce mixture and stir until it begins to boil. Add cornstarch and water mixture and continue to stir until the sauce thickens. Remove from the heat and mix in the cooked vegetables. Pour hot sauce and vegetables over the tofu on a serving plate. Serve immediately. Makes two servings.

재료(2인분) • 두부 한 모(1파운드), 물을 빼고 사방 1인치 크기로 자른다 • 전분 ½컵 • 카놀라유 ½컵 • 양배추잎 1개, 1×2인치로 썬다 • 당근 ¼개, 껍질을 벗기고 얇게 썬다 • 작은 오이 ½개, 얇게 썬다 소스 재료 • 채소국물(또는 물) 1컵 • 카놀라유 1큰술 • 다진 마늘 1작은술 • 다진 생강 1작은술 • 간장 2큰술 • 흑설탕 5큰술 • 식초 2큰술 • 전분 1큰술 + 물 1큰술, 잘 섞어둔다 전분을 뺀 소스 재료를 잘 섞어놓는다.

작은 그릇에 전분을 넣고 썰어 준비해둔 두부를 넣어 꼼꼼하게 전분을 묻힌다. 중간 불로 달군 팬에 카놀라유를 넉넉히 넣고 전분을 묻힌 두부를 서로 닿지 않게 놓아 겉이 노릇하도록 바삭하게 지져낸다. 다시 팬을 달궈 남은 기름에 준비해둔 채소를 넣어 약 1분간 살짝 볶아낸다. 두꺼운 냄비에 섞어둔 소스 재료를 넣고 저으면서 끓인다. 소스가 끓기 시작하면 물에 풀어둔 전분을 넣고 저으면서 끓여 꺼룩하게 만든다. 불을 끄고 볶아둔 채소를 넣어 섞는다. 접시에 튀긴 두부를 놓고 그 위에 뜨거운 소스를 부어낸다.

Potato and Zucchini Pancakes 감자호박전

In the summertime in Korea, the potatoes are plentiful so people often make potato pancakes to use up their reserves. The pancakes are essentially the Korean equivalent of latkes or hashbrowns, and are usually served with a dipping sauce made of sugar, vinegar and soy sauce. *Cook's Note: To keep potatoes from oxidizing, either put them in a bowl of water, or simply mix everything together as quickly as possible, cooking the pancakes right away.

Ingredients
• 2 large potatoes, peeled • ½ cup all-purpose flour
• ¼ teaspoon sea salt • ½ zucchini, shredded
• 1 mini red bell pepper, shredded
• ½ cup canola oil for cooking

Grate the potatoes into a large bowl and add flour and salt, mixing well. Then add zucchini and red pepper and combine. Heat 3 tablespoons of canola oil in large non-stick skillet over medium high heat. Spoon 1 tablespoon of the potato mixture into the pan and flatten with a spatula. Reduce the heat to medium and cook until golden brown, about 2 minutes on each side. Repeat with the rest of the potato mixture, adding more oil as needed. Makes two servings.

재료(2인분) • 큰 감자 2개, 껍질을 벗긴다 • 밀가루 ½컵 • 바다소금 ¼작은술 • 호박 ½개, 채 썬다 • 홍고추 1개, 채 썬다 • 카놀라유 ½컵(부침용)

감자를 강판에 갈아 재빨리 밀가루와 소금을 넣어 잘 섞는다.(감자는 갈아두면 검게 변하므로 물에 담가두거나 밀가루와 소금에 버무려두어야 갈변현상을 막을 수 있다.) 반죽에 채 썰어둔 호박과 붉은 고추를 넣고 잘 섞어 반죽을 완성한다. 달군 팬에 기름을 3큰술 정도 두르고 반죽을 1큰술씩 놓아 동글납작하게 펴서 노릇하게 앞뒤로 지져낸다. 새로 반죽을 놓을 때마다 기름을 둘러가며 지져낸다.

Cold Spicy Soba Noodles 냉모밀비빔국수

This noodle salad is a perfect meal for hot weather. The cold noodles are spicy and flavorful, and the vegetables are crunchy and fresh. It is just the type of thing you want to eat in the summertime with a large glass of iced tea. This salad is also great for packed lunches because it keeps well in the refrigerator and comes together in a matter of minutes. Just be sure to keep the dressing separate from the rest of the salad until just before eating in order to keep the noodles from getting too soggy.

Ingredients

- 2 bundles soba noodles
- I cup green cabbage, thinly sliced
- I cup snow peas, steamed and cut into thin strips
- 3 red radishes, cut into thin strips
- ½ cucumber, cut into thin strips

Ingredients for Sauce

- I ½ tablespoon gochujang (Korean hot pepper paste)
- I tablespoon sugar
- I tablespoon rice vinegar
- I tablespoon sesame oil
- 2 teaspoons toasted sesame seeds
- ½ teaspoon garlic, minced
- I tablespoon green onion, minced

Mix together all of the ingredients for the sauce and set aside. Cook soba noodles according to directions on the package and rinse with cold water, draining well. In a large bowl, combine cooked soba noodles, green cabbage, snow peas, red radishes, and cucumber. Add sauce, toss to combine and serve immediately. Makes two servings.

재료(2인분) • 모밀국수 2인분 • 채 썬 양배추 1컵 • 스노피 1컵, 데쳐서 채 썬다 • 래디시 3개, 채 썬다 • 오이 ½개, 채 썬다 비빔장 • 고추장 1 ½큰술 • 설탕 1큰술 • 식초 1큰술 • 참기름 1큰술 • 볶은 깨 2작은술 • 다진 마늘 ½작은술 • 다진 파 1큰술 비빔장 재료들을 잘 섞어둔다.

끓는 물에 모밀국수를 삶아 찬물에 헹구어 물기를 빼두고, 큰 그릇에 국수, 채 썬 양배추, 스노피, 래디시, 오이와 비빔장을 넣어 비벼서 낸다.

index

Kye Kim's Simply Delicious One Course Meals
케이 킴의 손쉽고 맛깔스러운 원 코스요리

Text Copyright ⓒ Kye Kim 2012
Photo Copyright ⓒ Kye Kim 2012
이 책의 모든 레시피, 사진, 요리법은 저작권법에 따라 보호를 받습니다.

초판인쇄　2012년 4월 1일
초판발행　2012년 4월 10일

지은이　케이킴
펴낸이　김정순
책임편집　이은정
디자인　김리영
마케팅　김보미 임정진

펴낸곳　(주)북하우스 퍼블리셔스
출판등록　1997년 9월 23일 제406-2003-055호
주소　121-840 서울시 마포구 서교동 395-4 선진빌딩 6층
전자우편　editor@bookhouse.co.kr
홈페이지　www.bookhouse.co.kr
전화번호　02-3144-3123
팩스　02-3144-3121

ISBN 978-89-5605-569-5 13590

이 도서의 국립중앙도서관 출판시도서목록(CIP)는 e-CIP홈페이지(http://www.nl.go.kr/ecip/default.php)에서
이용하실 수 있습니다.(CIP제어번호:CIP2012001364)